Published by Aperitifs Publishing Company

Published by Aperitifs Publishing Company
Santa Rosa, California

Copyright: October 2024

Compiled & Published by John C. Burton
johncburton@msn.com
707-523-1611

ISBN: 979-8-218-53355-7
Library of Congress Number: 2024921913

Printed in the United States of America

Every attempt has been made to provide accurate information on the following subjects.

FRONT COVER ACKNOWLEDGEMENTS

BARTLETT GINGER ALE L. E. McMAHAN & SONS TRADE MARK	John C. Burton Collection
BENECIA STEAM SODA WORKS GUSTAV GNAUCK	Steve & Christie Curtiss Collection
CROCKETT SODA WORKS CROCKETT, CAL.	Steve & Christie Curtiss Collection
F. O. BRANDT HEALDSBURG, CAL.	John C. Burton Collection
HALF MOON BAY SODA WATER CO. HALF MOON BAY CAL.	Steve & Christie Curtiss Collection
JACKSON'S NAPA SODA	John C. Burton Collection
KERN COUNTY BOTTLING WORKS	Steve & Christie Curtiss Collection
LIVERMORE SODA WORKS (LAMB) LIVERMORE CAL.	Steve & Christie Curtiss Collection
BRADLEY SODA WATER (Eagle) SAN DIEGO, CAL.	Rick Hall Collection

REAR COVER ACKNOWLEDGEMENTS

BAKERSFIELD VLASNIK BOTTLING WORKS	Steve & Christie Curtiss Collection
GOLDEN WEST SODA WORKS SAN FRANCISCO, CAL.	John C. Burton Collection
MASON SAUSALITO GINGERALE	Dan Brown Collection
ROSE CITY SODA WORKS SANTA ROSA, CAL.	Steve & Christie Curtiss Collection
SAN ANSELMO BOTTLING CO. SAN RAFAEL, CAL.	John C. Burtron Collection
WILSON MF'G HIGH GRADE CARBONATED DRINKS SACRAMENTO, CAL.	Steve & Christie Curtiss

ADDITIONAL CONTRIBUTORS TO THIS EDITION
Helm &DeAnna Jordt – Merle Avila - Dan Brown – Rick Siri - Gary Christensen – Rick Hall
Mike Rouse – Dale Mlasko - David W. Garcia – Eddie Kuskie – Mike Ertmoed -Bruce Silva
Bob Voegtly & Darrell Paul

CALIFORNIA EMBOSSED CROWN TOP BOTTLES
Volume 1

California Embossed Soda Bottles is attempted to bring the often-over-looked embossed crown top bottles forward to be recognized and appreciated by collectors.

The suggestion of this book was brought to me by Steve Bava and by Steve & Christie Curtiss. It started off as a book I enjoyed doing but turned to sadness with the Corral Fire in Tracy that consumed Steve & Christie Curtiss' home and fabulous collections of blob top, gravitating stopper, hutch, crown top bottles, beer cans, arrowheads and general antiques that were throughout their home.

They had collected everything imaginal with pride of every California hutch known except three.

Dale Chase, North Bay Bottle Club Member, and I spent many Saturdays with Steve & Christie talking about bottles. It is fortunate that I still have many photos of their collections that I took on my cell phone "unknowingly" becoming reference for their insurance purposes.

Who could ever forget this wall of California Hutches.

To Steve & Christie who have become great friends of myself and Dale Chase we dedicate this book.

AETNA SPRINGS
Face: AETNA
              MINERAL
              WATER
Color: Aqua
Rarity: Scarce
Value: $_____
Steve Bava Collection

ALAMEDA
Face: ALAMEDA
            Hands Shaking
            SODA WATER CO.
            THIS BOTTLE NOT SOLD
Color: Aqua
Rarity: Scarce
Value: $_____
Steve Bava Collection

ALAMEDA
Skirt: ALAMEDA SODA WATER
              ALAMEDA CAL.
Color: Clear
Rarity:
Value: $_____
Steve & Christie Curtiss Collection

ALDER GLEN
Face: ALDER GLEN
                MINERAL
                SPRINGS
Back: ALDER
                GLEN
                A NATURAL
                MINERAL WATER
                THIS BOTTLE IS
                NEVER SOLD
Color: Aqua
Rarity: Very Rare
Value: $_____
John Burton Collection

AMADOR
Face: AMADOR CO.
           SODA WORKS
Color: Aqua
Rarity: Rare
Value: $_____
Image

AMADOR
Face: AMADOR CO.
              N
           SODA WORKS
Color: Sun Colored Amethyst
Rarity: Rare
Value: $_____
Steve Bava Collection

AMADOR

Face: AMADOR COUNTY
        L. BROS.
        SODA WORKS
Color: Aqua
Rarity: Rare
Value: $_____
Steve Bava Collection

ANAHEIM

Face: ORANGE COUNTY SODA WORKS
            ANAHEIM
Color: Aqua
Rarity: Rare
Value: $_____
Marlon Christmann Collection

ANAHEIM

McCREARY & SWANSON
ANAHEIM, CAL.

Color: Clear
Rarity: Rare
Value: $_____

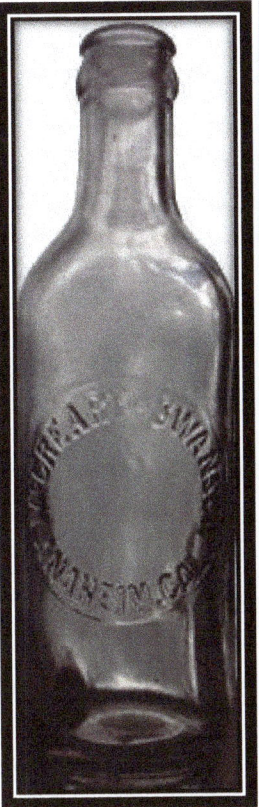

ANGELS
Face: ANGELS BREWERY
AND
SODA WORKS
E.F. HUBLER
PROP.
Color: Light Purple
Rarity: Rare
Value $_____
Steve Bava Collection

ANGELS
Face: G. W.
       ANGELS
Color: Aqua
Rarity: Very Rare
Value: $_____
Steve Bava Collection

ANGELS
Face: G. W.
       ANGELS
Color: Amber
Rarity: Extremely Rare
Value: $_____
Bava

ANGELS
Face: H. & W.
       ANGELS
Color: Aqua
Rarity: Unique
Value: $_____
Image

ANGELS
Bottom: Embossed on bottom
       E. F. H.
       ANGELS
Color: Aqua
Rarity:
Value: $_____
Bava

ANGELS
Face: DAVY CROCKETT
          LIQUOR CO.
          ANGELS
Color: Aqua
Rarity: Very Scarce
Value: $_____
Steve & Christie Curtiss Collection

ANGELS
Face: MARTIN BROS.
          ANGELS
Color: Aqua
Rarity: Very Scarce
Value: $_____
Steve Bava Collection

ANGELS
Face: MORGAN & PACHE
            ANGELS
Color: Aqua
Rarity:
Value: $_____
Steve Bava Collection

ANGELS
Face: SEQUOIA
            SODA WORKS
            ANGELS
            CAL.
Color: Aqua
Rarity:
Value: $_____
Steve & Christie Curtiss Collection

ANGELS (In Box)
Face: SEQUOIA
        SODA WORKS
        ANGELS
        CAL.
Color: Light Green
Rarity:
Value: $_____
Gary Christensen Collection

ANTIOCH
Face: ANTIOCH
        SODA WORKS
        ANTIOCH, CAL.
Color: Aqua
Rarity: Scarce
Value: $_____
Steve & Christie Curtiss Collection

ANTIOCH
Face: ANTIOCH SODA WORKS
           ANTIOCH
              CAL.

Color: Aqua
Rarity: Common
Value: $_____
Steve Bava Collection

ARROYO GRANDE
Face: ARROYO GRANDE
          SODA WORKS
Color: Aqua
Rarity: Very rare
Value: $_____
Steve Bava Collection

AUBURN
Skirt: CONTENTS 8 OZ.
Bottom: A. W. KENISON CO.
                   AUBURN

Color: Aqua
Rarity: Common
Value: $_____
Steve & Christie Curtiss Collection

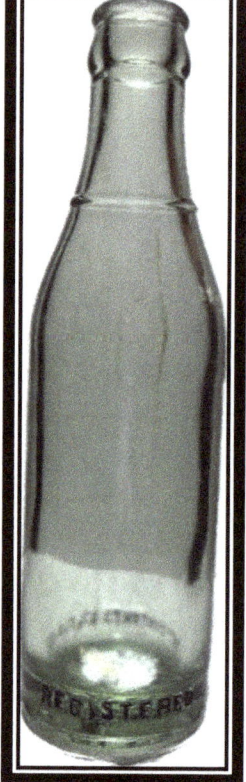

AUBURN
Bottom: A W. K. CO.
                   AUBURN
                          CAL.
Color: Aqua & Purple
Rarity: Semi Common
Value: $_____
Steve & Christie Curtiss Collection

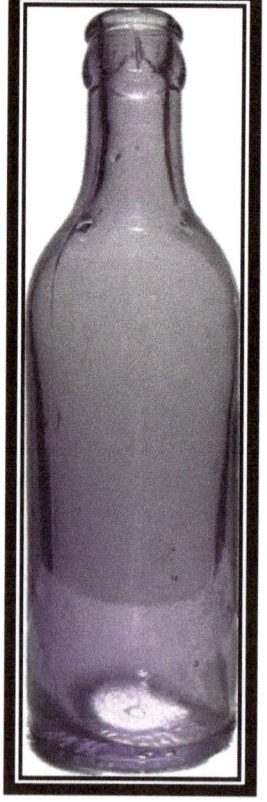

BAKERSFIELD
Face: BAKERSFIELD
           BOTTLING
           WORKS
Color: Aqua
Rarity: Scarce
Value: $_____
Steve Bava Collection

BAKERSFIELD
Face: BAKERSFIELD
           VLASNIK
           BOTTLING WORKS
Color: Green
Rarity: Rare
Value: $_____
Steve & Christie Curtiss Collection

BAKERSFIELD
Skirt: CAL. LEMONADE AND SELTZER CO.
Color: Aqua
Rarity: Rare
Value: $_____
Steve Bava Collection

BAKERSFIELD
Face: C.O.D.
           SODA WORKS
           BAKERSFIELD
Color: Light Purple
Rarity: Rare
Value: $_____
Steve Bava Collection

BAKERSFIELD

Face: KERN COUNTY
          BOTTLING WORKS
            BAKERSFIELD
               CAL.

Color: Aqua

Rarity: Scarce

Value: $_____

Marlon Christmann Collection

BAKERSFIELD

Face: KERN
          COUNTY
          BOTTLING
          WORKS

Color: Aqua

Rarity:

Value: $_____

Steve & Christie Curtiss Collection

BERKELEY
Face: ARTIC
           SODA WATER CO.
           BERKELEY
           CAL.
           BOTTLE NEVER SOLD
Base: 10-Sided Mug Base
Color: Aqua
Rarity: Rare
Value: $_____
Image

BERKELEY
Face: CRYSTAL DISTILLED
          PURE WATER CO.
          BERKELEY, CAL.
Color: Aqua
Rarity: Very Scarce
Value $_____
Steve Bava Collection

BERKELEY (Circle)
Face: REGESTERED
             PURE
             WATER
             CO.
       BERKELEY, CAL.

Color: Sun Colored Amethyst
Rarity:
Value: $_____
Steve Bava Collection

BENICIA
Face: BENICIA
          STEAM
      SODA WORKS
     GUSTAV GNAUCK
Color: Aqua
Rarity: Very Rare
Value: $_____
Steve & Christie Curtiss Collection

BISHOP
Face: INYO BOTTLING WORKS
        BISHOP, CALIF.
Color: Aqua
Rarity: Rare
Value: $_____
Steve & Christie Curtiss Collection

BISHOP
Face: INYO BOTTLING WORKS
        BISHOP, CALIF.
Color: Light Purple
Rarity: Very Rare
Value: $_____
Steve & Christie Curtiss Collection

CALISTOGA (Napa County)
Face: CALISTOGA BOTTLING WKS.
                C. MUSANTE
             CALISTOGA, CAL.
          Color: Aqua
Rarity: Extremely Rare
Value: $_____
John Burton Collection

CASTELLA
Face: CASTLE ROCK
Color: Amber
Rarity:
Value $_____
Steve Bava Collection

CASTELLA

Face: CASTLE ROCK
           N. M.
           SPRING CO.
           CASTELLA, CAL.

Color: Amber
Rarity: Extremely Rare
Value $_____
Steve Bava Collection

CASTELLA

Face: CASTLE ROCK
           SPRING CO.
           CASTELLA, CAL.

Color: Amber
Rarity: Extremely Rare
Value $_____
Steve Bava Collection

CHICO   (Embossed on bottom)
Bottom: C.S.W.
           CHICO, CAL.
Color: Aqua & Light Purple
Rarity:
Value: $_____
Left - Steve Bava Collection
Right Steve & Christie Curtiss

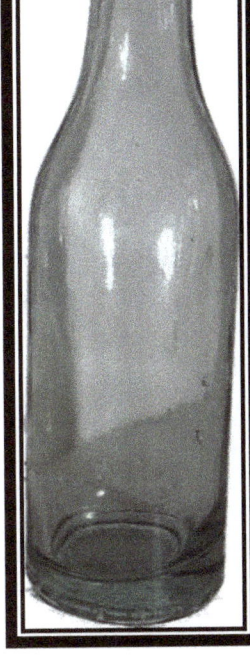

CHICO   (Embossed on Bottom)
Base: MILLER
          CHICO
Color: Aqua
Rarity:
Value: $_____
Steve Bava Collection

COLMA
Face: BALKAN
                SODA WORKS
                COLMA
                SAN MATEO CO.
                CAL.
Color: Aqua
Rarity: Very Rare
Value: $_____
Image

COLUSA
Face: J. W. DAVIS
             COLUSA, CAL.
Color: Amber
Rarity: Very Rare
Value: $_____
Steve Bava Collection

CONCORD

Face: CONCORD
                     <Eagle>
                SODA WORKS
        C. J. & R.H.T. in shield
            CONCORD, CAL

Color: Clear & Aqua
Rarity: Rare
Value $_____
Steve & Christie Curtiss Collection

CORNING

Face: C. I. & B .W.
            CORNING
               CAL.

Color: Sun Colored Amethyst
Rarity: Rare
Value $_____
Steve & Christie Curtiss Collection

CROCKETT
Face: CROCKETT
        SODA WORKS
        CROCKETT, CAL.
Color: Aqua
Rarity: Very Rare
Value: $_____
Steve & Christie Curtiss Collection

DIXON
Face: DIXON
Color: Aqua
Rarity: Scarce
Value $_____
Steve Bava Collection

DUNSMUIR (Half Circle)
Face: UPPER SODA
         DUNSMUIR
             CAL.
Color: Aqua
Rarity:
Value: $_____
Steve Bava Collection

DUNSMUIR
Face: UPPER SODA
         DUNSMUIR
             CAL.
Color: Aqua
Rarity:
Value: $_____
Steve Bava Collection

DUNSMUIR (Vertical)
Face: UPPER SODA MINERAL SPRINGS CO.
                   DUNSMUIR, CAL.
Color: Aqua
Rarity:
Value: $_____
Image

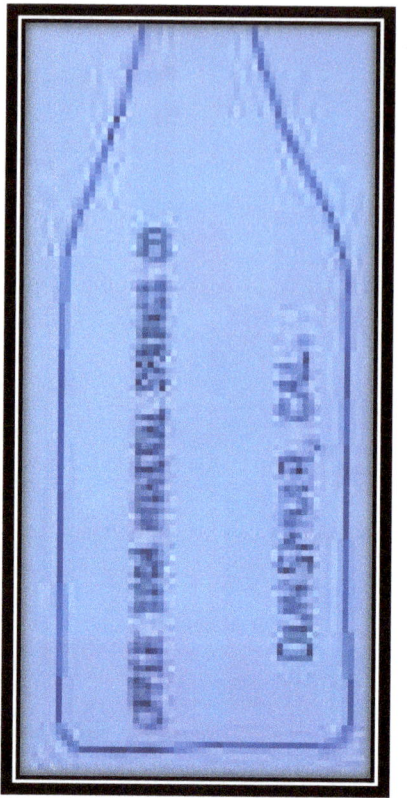

ELMHURST
Face: ELMHURST
                <E>
        SODA WATER CO.
Color: Aqua
Rarity: Common
Value: $_____
John Burton Collection

ETNA
Face: G. KAPPLER
          ETNA BREWERY
            ETNA, CAL.
Color: Aqua
Rarity: Rare
Value: $_____
Steve Bava Collection

ETNA SPRINGS
Face: ETNA
          MINERAL
          WATER
Color: Aqua
Rarity: Common
Value: $_____
Steve Bava Collection

ETNA AREA
Face: I-ADORA-A
           NATURAL
           MINERAL
           WATER
Color: Amber
Rarity:
Value: $_____
Steve Bava Collection

EUREKA
Face: DELANEY & YOUNG
           EUREKA, CAL.
Color: Aqua
Rarity:
Value: $_____
Steve Bava Collection

EUREKA
Face: DELANEY & YOUNG
            EUREKA, CAL.
Color: Aqua
Rarity:
Value: $_____
Steve Bava Collection

EUREKA
Face: MONROE
        CIDER & VINEGAR CO.
            EUREKA,
              CAL.
Color: Aqua
Rarity:
Value: $_____
Steve Bava Collection

EUREKA (Skirt Embossed)
Shirt: MONROE'S GINGER ALE
Color: Aqua
Rarity:
Value: $_____
Steve Bava Collection

EUREKA
Face: WILSON'S
          SODA WORKS
          EUREKA, CAL.
Color: Aqua
Rarity:
Value: $_____
John Burton Collection

EUREKA & SANTA BARBARA
Face: EAGLE
         SODA WORKS
         C. F. RILEY
Color: Aqua & Clear
Rarity: Very Scarce
Value: $_____
Steve Bava Collection

FOREST HILL
Face: FOREST HILL
         ELECTRIC CO.
         FOREST HILL
         CAL.
Color: Aqua
Rarity: Extremely Rare
Value: $_____
Steve Bava Collection

FORT BRAGG
Face: STANDARD
            BOTTLING CO.
            FORT BRAGG
Color: Clear
Rarity:
Value: $_____
Darrell Paul Collection

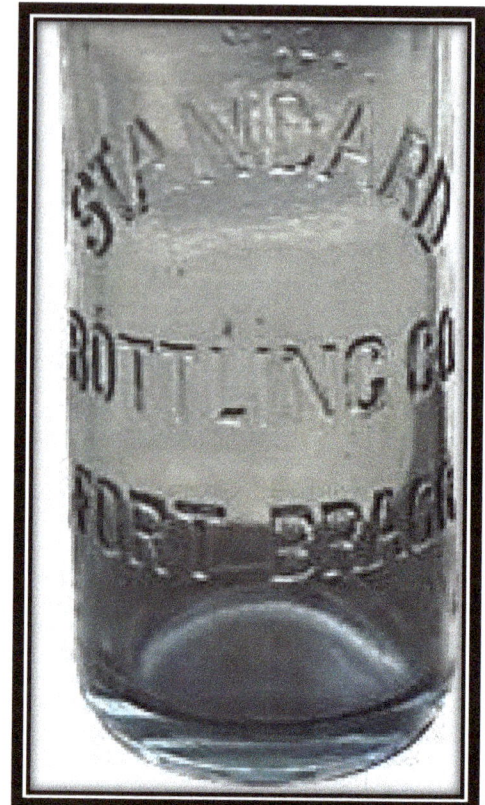

FORT BRAGG
Face: STANDARD
            8 OZ. SODA
            WATER
Color: Clear
Rarity:
Value: $_____
Darrell Paul Collection

FREMONT
Face: FREMONT BOTTLING WORKS
Color: Aqua
Rarity:
Value: $_____
Steve Bava Collection

FRESNO
Face: BORELLO BROS.
         TRADE B. B. MARK
         FRESNO CAL.
Color: Aqua
Rarity: Common
Value: $_____
Steve & Christie Curtiss Collection

FRESNO
Face: Blank – Base Embossed
Bottom: BB (Borello Bros.)
         FRESNO
Color: Sun Colored Amethyst
Rarity: Semi Common
Value: $_____
Steve Bava Collection

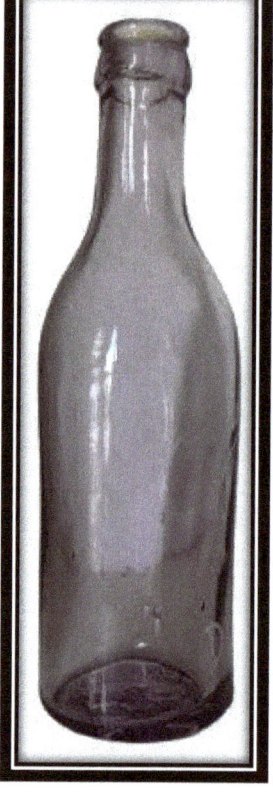

FRESNO
Embossed on bottom
Bottom: CALIFORNIA SODA WORKS
         FRESNO
Color: Aqua
Rarity:
Value: $ _____
Steve & Christie Curtiss Collection

FRESNO
Embossed on bottom
Bottom CRYSTAL SODA WKS.
J M
FRESNO, CAL.
Color: Aqua
Rarity:
Value: $_____
Steve Bava Collection

FRESNO
Face: JACOB RICHTER
FRESNO
CAL.
Color: Amber
Rarity: Rare
Value: $_____
Steve & Christie Curtiss Collection

FRESNO
Embossed on bottom
Bottom   JACOB RICHTER CO.
                FRESNO
                  CAL.

Color: Aqua
Rarity:
Value: $_____
Steve & Christie Curtiss Collection

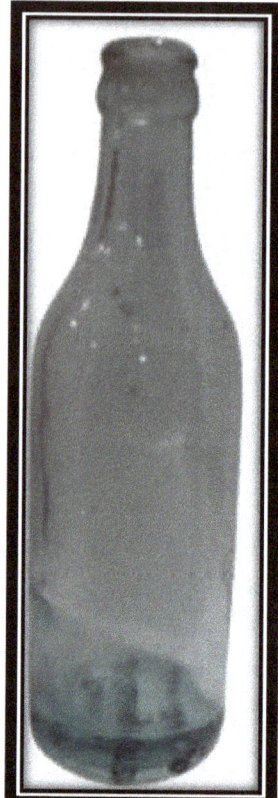

FRESNO
Embossed on bottom
Bottom   JACOB RICHTER CO.
                (Star)
                FRESNO
                  CAL.

Color: Aqua
Rarity:
Value: $_____
Steve & Christie Curtiss Collection

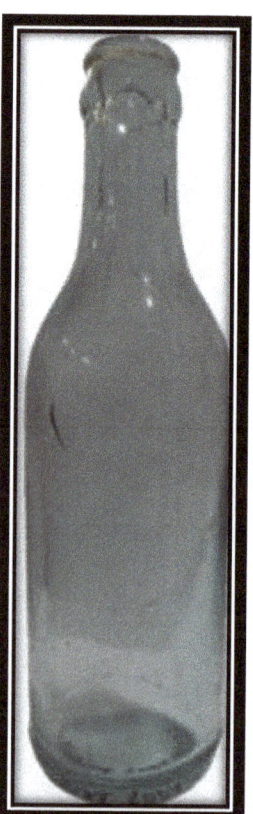

FRESNO
Face: RICHTER'S
            BOTTLING WORKS
              FRESNO, CAL
Color: Aqua & Clear
Rarity:
Value: $_____
Steve Bava Collection

FRESNO (Arch)
Face: MORIMOTO SODA WORKS
              TRADE
              < T M >
              MARK
             FRESNO, CAL.
Color: Aqua
Rarity:
Value: $_____
Steve & Christie Curtiss Collection

FRESNO
(Arch)
Face: MORIMOTO SODA WORKS
                    TRADE
                    < T M >
                    MARK
                FRESNO, CAL.
Color: Sun Colored Amethyst
Rarity:
Value: $_____
Steve Bava Collection

FRESNO
Bottom: PARLIER
                SODA WORKS
Color: Aqua
Rarity:
Value: $_____
Steve Bava Collection

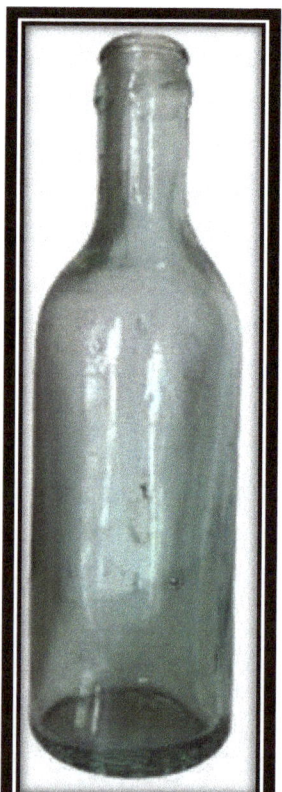 

FRESNO
Face: SAN JOAQUIN SODA WATER WORKS
                    <S. J. S. W.>
                      FRESNO
                        CAL.

Color: Aqua
Rarity:
Value: $_____
Marlon Christmann Collection

(Full Diamond)

FRESNO
Face: SAN JOAQUIN SODA WATER WORKS
                     S. J. S. W.
                      FRESNO
                        CAL.

Color: Aqua
Rarity:
Value: $_____
Steve & Christie Curtiss Collection

GILROY
Face: PIONEER
         SODA WORKS
         GILROY
Color: Aqua
Rarity:
Value: $_____
John Burton Collection

GRASS VALLEY
Face: R. H. WILLIAMS
         GRASS VALLEY
Color: Aqua
Rarity:
Value: $_____
Steve Bava Collection

GRASS VALLEY
Face: R. H. WILLIAMS
        GRASS VALLEY
Color: Apple Green
Rarity:
Value: $_____

GRASS VALLEY
Face: R. H. WILLIAMS
            GRASS VALLEY
        NET CONTENTS 7½ OZS.
Color: Clear
Rarity:
Value: $_____
Gary Christensen Collection

GRIDLEY
Face: GRIDLEY ICE
              AND
         SODA WORKS
         GRIDLEY, CAL.
Color: Aqua
Rarity:
Value: $_____
Marlon Christmann Collection

HALF MOON BAY
Face: HALF MOON BAY
         Half Moon logo
         SODA WATER CO.

Color: Aqua
Rarity:
Value: $_____
Image

HALF MOON BAY
Face: HALF MOON BAY
          SODA
        WATER
          CO.
      HALF MOON BAY, CAL.
Color: Aqua
Rarity:
Value: $_____
Steve Bava Collection

HALF MOON BAY (Sloping Shoulders)
Face: HALF MOON BAY
      SODA WATER CO.
      HALF MOON BAY
         CAL.
Color: Aqua
Rarity:
Value: $_____
Steve & Christie Curtiss Collection

HALF MOON BAY (Square Shoulders)
Face: HALF MOON BAY
            SODA WATER CO.
            HALF MOON BAY
                 CAL.
Color: Aqua
Rarity:
Value: $_____
Steve Bava Collection

HANFORD
Face: HANFORD
            ICE
          COMPANY
Color: Aqua
Rarity:
Value: $_____
Steve & Christie Curtiss Collection

HANFORD
Face: HANFORD ICE CO.
           HANFORD
              CAL.
Color: Aqua
Rarity:
Value: $_____
Steve Bava Collection

HANFORD
Face: HANFORD
           SODA WORKS
             J. S.
Color: Aqua
Rarity:
Value: $_____
Steve & Christie Curtiss Collection

HANFORD (Fancy script)
Face: HANFORD
        SODA WORKS
        J. S.
Color: Aqua
Rarity:
Value: $_____
Steve Bava Collection

HAYWARD
Face: HAYWARDS
        SODA WORKS
        COMPANY
Color: Aqua
Rarity:
Value: $_____
Steve & Christie Curtiss Collection

HAYWARD
Face: HAYWARDS
        S. J. SIMONS
        SODA WORKS
Color: Aqua
Rarity:
Value: $_____
Steve Bava Collection

HAYWARD
Face: HAYWARDS
        SODA WORKS
        S. J. SIMONS
Color: Clear
Rarity:
Value: $_____
Steve & Christie Curtiss Collection

HAYWARD (Circle)
Face: HAYWARDS
         SODA WORKS
         S. J. SIMONS
Color: Aqua
Rarity:
Value: $_____
Steve Bava Collection

HEALDSBURG
Face: F. O. BRANDT
         HEALDSBURG
            CAL.
Bottom: B
Color: Aqua
Rarity: Semi Common
Value: $_____
John Burton Collection

HEALDSBURG
Face: F. B.
          HEALDSBURG
            CAL.
Color: Aqua
Rarity: Very Rare
Value: $_____
John Burton Collection

Thanks Steve. JB

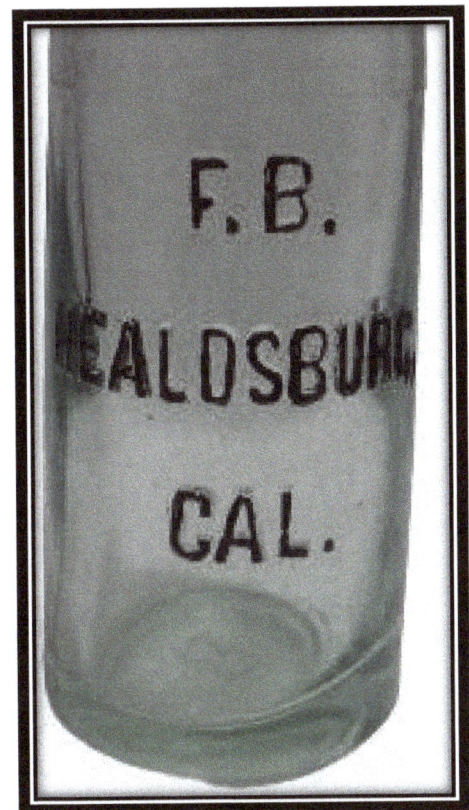

HEMET
Face: HEMET SODA WORKS
            HEMET
            CAL.
Color: Aqua
Rarity:
Value: $_____
Eddie Kuskie Collection

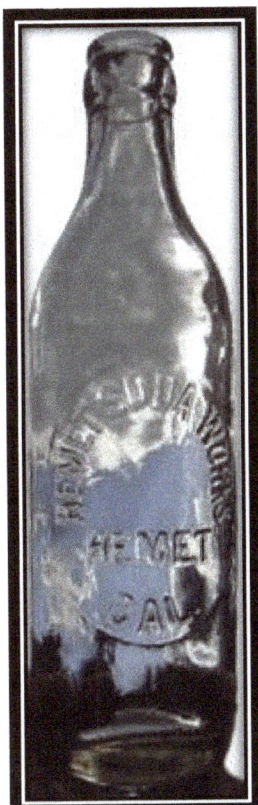

HEMET
Face: HEMET
                 SODA WORKS
                 HEMET, CALIF.
Color: Aqua
Rarity:
Value: $_____
Eddie Kuskie Collection

HOLLISTER
Face: HOLLISTER
                 SODA WORKS
                 HOLLISTER, CAL.
Color: Aqua
Rarity:
Value: $_____
Steve Bava Collection

HOLLISTER

Face: HOLLISTER SODA WORKS
NET CONTENTS
8 OZ.

Color: Aqua
Rarity:
Value: $_____
Steve & Christie Curtiss Collection

HOLLYWOOD

Face: VALLEY SPRINGS & SODA
WORKS
HOLLYWOOD
CALIFORNIA

Color: Aqua
Rarity: Extremely Rare
Value: _____
Steve & Christie Curtiss Collection

IONE
Face: IONE ICE & SODA WORKS
               L A P
           IONE, CAL.
Color: Clear
Rarity: Scarce
Value: $_____
Steve & Christie Curtiss Collection

 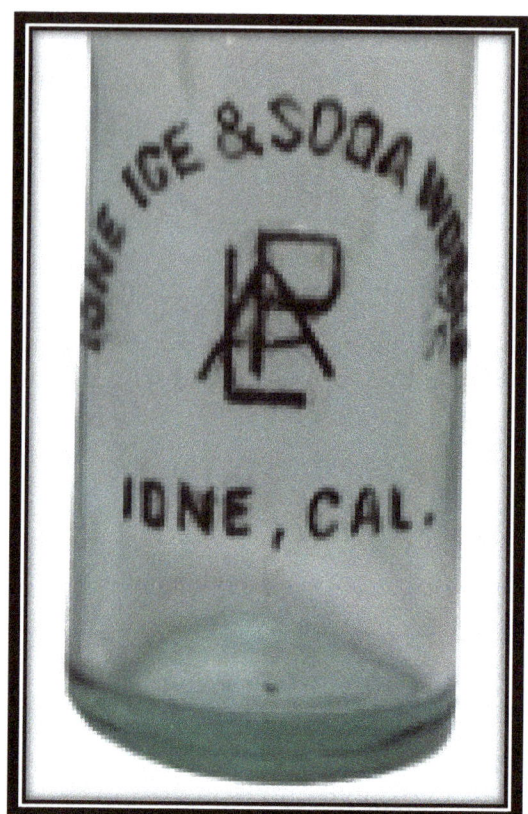

JACKSON
Face: J. T. SCHERRER
           JACKSON
Color: Apple Green
Rarity: Common
Value: $_____
Steve Bava Collection

JACKSON
Face: JACKSON BOTTLING
   P. & G.
   WORKS
Color: Aqua
Rarity: Scarce
Value: $_____
Steve & Christie Curtiss Collection

JACKSON
Face: JACKSON BOTTLING
   P.
   WORKS
Color: Aqua
Rarity: Scarce
Value: $_____
Steve Bava Collection

JACKSON
Face: JACKSON BOTTLING
               Fancy P
               WORKS
Color: Aqua
Rarity: Scarce
Value: $_____
Steve Bava Collection

JACKSON
Face: JACKSON BOTTLING
               P.
               WORKS
Color: Sun Color Amethyst
Rarity: Scarce
Value: $_____
Steve Bava Collection

JACKSON
Face: JACKSON
               P. & T
          BOTTLING WORKS
Color: Aqua
Rarity: Scarce
Value: $_____
Steve Bava Collection

JACKSON
Face: JACKSON BOTTLING
               P. & T
          WORKS
Color: Clear
Rarity: Scarce
Value: $_____
Steve & Christie Curtiss Collection

JACKSON
Face: JOHN STROHM
         JACKSON, CAL.
Color: Clear
Rarity:
Value: $_____
Steve & Christie Curtiss Collection

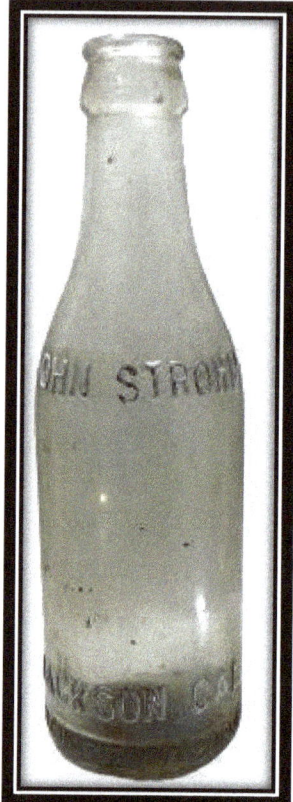

KENNETT
Face: KENNETT
         BOTTLING WORKS
         J. D. COOK & SON
               PROPS.
Color: Aqua
Rarity: Extremely Rare
Value: $_____
Steve Bava Collection

KERN
Face: STAR SODA WORKS
                    ★
            KERN, CAL.
Color: Aqua
Rarity:
Value: $_____
Steve & Christie Curtiss Collection

KERN
Face: KERN
            COUNTY
            BOTTLING
            WORKS
Color: Aqua
Rarity:
Value: $_____
Steve & Christie Curtiss Collection

Also shown in Bakersfield heading

LAKE COUNTY
Face: BARTLETT
            GINGER ALE
            L.E. McMAHAN & SONS
            Trade mark
Vertical Embossing
Color: Aqua
Rarity: Rare
Value: $_____
John Burton Collection

LAKE COUNTY
Face: HIGHLAND
            MINERAL
            WATER
Reverse: HIGHLAND
            MINERAL
            WATER
Color: Aqua
Rarity: Very Rare
Value: $_____
Rick Siri Collection

LAKE COUNTY
Face: HIGHLAND (Vertical)
Reverse: NATURAL
          MINERAL
          WATER
 Color: Aqua
Rarity: Very Rare
Value: $_____
Steve Bava Collection

LAKE COUNTY (Vertical Embossing)
Face: ALLEN SPRINGS CO.
               LAKE CO.
               CALIFORNIA
Color: Aqua
Rarity:
Value: $_____
Steve Bava Collection

LIVERMORE
Face: LIVERMORE SODA WORKS
                Lamb
             LIVERMORE
                CAL.

Color: Aqua
Rarity: Rare
Value: $_____
Steve & Christie Curtiss Collection

LIVERMORE
Face: LIVERMORE SODA WORKS
             LIVERMORE
                    CAL.

Color: Aqua
Rarity: Rare
Value: $_____
            Half Circle
Steve Bava Collection

LIVERMORE

Face: LIVERMORE SODA WORKS
                 LSW
             LIVERMORE
                CAL.

Color: Aqua
Rarity: Very Rare
Value: $_____
          Half Circle
Steve Bava Collection

LONG BEACH

Face: SUPERIOR
          BOTTLING WORKS
          LONG BEACH CAL.

Color: Clear
Rarity: Rare
Value: $_____
Steve & Christie Curtiss Collection

LONG BEACH
Face: **PEOPLES**
                ICE
                &
        COLD STORAGE
                CO.
      LONG BEACH
Color: Aqua
Rarity: Rare
Value: $_____
Eddie Kuskie Collection

LOS ANGELES
Face: **ACME BOTTLING**
                WORKS
            LOS ANGELES
Color: Aqua
Rarity:
Value: $_____
David W. Garcia Collection

LOS ANGELES
Face: ALOHA BOTTLING WORKS
                W. & S.
            LOS ANGELES
                CAL.

Color: Aqua
Rarity: Very Rare
Value: $_____
Steve Bava Collection

LOS ANGELES
ace: CRYSTAL BOTTLING
                CBCo.
        COMPANY LOS ANGELES

Color: Aqua
Rarity:
Value: $_____
Steve & Christie Curtiss Collection

LOS ANGELES
Face: CASCADE SODA WORKS
             PEVERLY
              BROS.
             PROPS.
         LOS ANGELES
Color: Sun Colored Amethyst
Rarity:
Value: $_____
Steve Bava Collection

LOS ANGELES
Face: EXCELSIOR
         SODA WORKS
           LOS
        ANGELES CAL.
Color: Aqua
Rarity:
Value: $_____
Steve Bava Collection

LOS ANGELES
Face: F. A. HEIM'S
            BOTTLING WORKS
Color: Aqua
Rarity:
Value: $_____
Steve Bava Collection

LOS ANGELES
Face: ELYSIAN SPRING
            WATER CO.
            LOS ANGELES
Color: Aqua
Rarity:
Value: $_____
Steve & Christie Curtiss Collection

LOS ANGELES
Face: HONEY CHAMPAGNE
V. H. Co.
LOS ANGELES
CALIF.
Color: Aqua
Rarity: Extremely Rare
Value: $_____
Eddie Kuskie Collection

LOS ANGELES
Face: HYGEIA
MINERAL WATER
CO.
LOS ANGELES
CAL.
Color: Aqua
Rarity:
Value: $_____
Steve Bava Collection

LOS ANGELES
Face: LOS ANGELES
⭐
SODA WORKS
Base: THIS BOTTLE IS REGISTERED
NOT TO BE SOLD
Color: Aqua
Rarity: Common
Value: $_____
Steve & Christie Curtiss Collection

LOS ANGELES
Face: LOS ANGELES
⭐
SODA WORKS
Base: THIS BOTTLE IS REGISTERED
NOT TO BE SOLD
Color: Aqua

Rarity: Common
Value: $_____
Steve Bava Collection

LOS ANGELES

Skirt: LOS ANGELES ICE & COLD STORAGE
                  LOS ANGELES

Color: Aqua
Rarity:
Value: $_____
Steve Bava Collection

LOS ANGELES

Face: NEW YORK
         BOTTLING WORKS
         LOS ANGELES
            CAL.

Color: Aqua
Rarity:
Value: $_____
Steve Bava Collection

LOS ANGELES
Face: NEW YORK
             BOTTLING WORKS
             LOS ANGELES
Color: Aqua
Rarity:
Value: $_____
Steve Bava Collection

LOS ANGELES
Face: IDEAL BOTTLING WORKS
             LOS ANGELES, CAL.
Color: Clear
Rarity: Common
Value: $ _____
Steve & Christie Curtiss Collection

LOS ANGELES

Face: PROPERTY OF THE
PURITAS
L. A. L. & C. S. CO
LOS ANGELES
BOTTLE NOT TO BE SOLD.

Color: Amber

Rarity:

Value: $_____

Steve Bava Collection

LOS ANGELES

Face: THE ICE & COLD
STORAGE CO.
PURITAS
OF
LOS ANGELES, CAL.
THIS BOTTLE
IS NOT SOLD

Color: Aqua

Rarity:

Value: $_____

Steve Bava Collection

LOS ANGELES
Skirt: LOS ANGELES
          ICE & COLD STORAGE CO.
           BOTTLE IS NOT SOLD
Color: Aqua
Rarity:
Value: $_____
Steve Bava Collection

LOS ANGELES
Face: RAMONA
          BOTTLING
           WORKS
            LOS ANGELES, CAL.
Color: Aqua
Rarity:
Value: $_____
Steve & Christie Curtiss Collection

LOS ANGELES
Face: RAMONA
            LOS ANGELES
            BOTTLING   WORKS
Color: Clear
Rarity:
Value: $_____
Eddie Kuskie Collection

LOS ANGELES & VENTURA
Face: REGISTERED
        SHAW OF CALIFORNIA
           SFB (Logo)
          HIGH GRADE
           BEVERAGES
      LOS ANGELES & VENTURA
Color: Clear
Rarity: Rare
Value: $_____
Steve & Christie Curtiss Collection

LOS ANGELES

Face: WHITE STAR
          SODA WORKS
          LOS ANGELES, CAL.

Color: Aqua

Rarity:

Value: $_____

Steve Bava Collection

LOS BANOS

Face: LOS BANOS
          I. B.
          SODA WORKS

Color: Aqua

Rarity: Scarce

Value: $_____

Steve Bava Collection
      (Full Circle)

LOS BANOS (Circle)
Face: LOS BANOS
          I & B
          SODA WORKS
Color: Aqua
Rarity: Common
Value: $_____
Steve Bava Collection

LOS BANOS
Face: LOS BANOS
          IACOPI & BROS.
          SODA WORKS
Color: Aqua
Rarity: Very Scarce
Value: $_____
Steve Bava Collection

LOS BANOS
Face: LOS BANOS
        SODA WORKS
Color: Aqua
Rarity:
Value: $_____
Steve Bava Collection

LOS BANOS
Bottom: LOS BANOS SODA WORKS
         LOS BANOS, CAL.
Color: Aqua
Rarity:
Value: $_____
Steve Bava Collection

LOS GATOS

Face: LOS GATOS SODA WKS.
        L. & M.
        LOS GATOS CAL.

Color: Aqua
Rarity: Rare
Value: $_____
Steve & Christie Curtiss Collection

LOS GATOS

Face: LOS GATOS SODA WKS
        (Cat)
        LOS GATOS, CAL.
        NET CONTENTS 8 FL. OZS.

Color: Green
Rarity: Very Rare
Value: $_____
Steve & Christie Curtiss Collection

MADERA
    BORELLO & PORTER
        MADERA
Color: Aqua
Rarity:
Value: $_____
Steve & Christie Curtiss Collection

MADERA
Face: J. G. PORTER
        BOTTLING WORKS
        MADERA, CAL.
Color: Aqua
Rarity: Scarce
Value: $_____
Steve & Christie Curtiss Collection

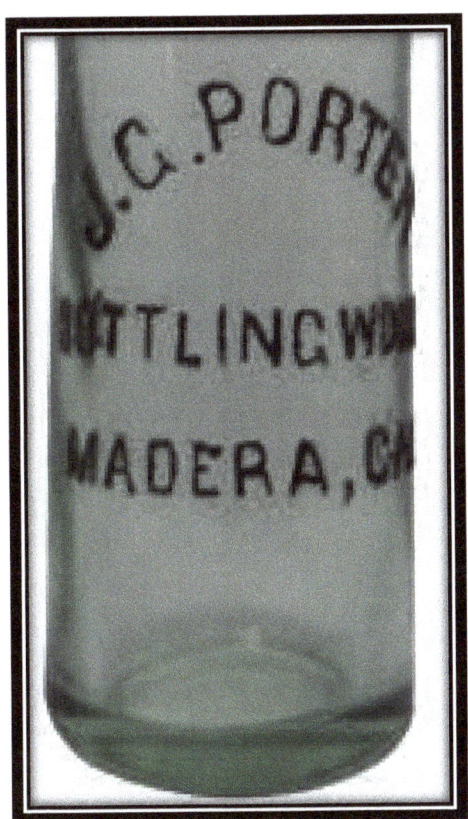

MARTINEZ
Face: ALHAMBRA
              GINGER ALE
              ALHAMBRA
              NATURAL
         MINERAL WATER CO.
              MARTINEZ,
                 CAL.

Color: Aqua
Rarity: Scarce
Value: $_____
Steve Bava Collection

MARTINEZ
Face: ALHAMBRA
           MINERAL WATER
Skirt: BOTTLED AT SPRINGS
Color: Aqua
Rarity: Scarce
Value: $_____
Steve Bava Collection

MARTINEZ

A.N.M.W. CO.
TRADE MARK
REGISTERED
NET CONTENTS 7 OZ.
"ALHAMBRA"
MARTINEZ, CAL.

Color: Aqua
Rarity: Very Scarce
Value: $_____
Steve Bava Collection

MARTINEZ

A.N.M.W. CO.
TRADE MARK
REGISTERED
"ALHAMBRA"
MARTINEZ, CAL.

Color: Aqua
Rarity: Very Scarce
Value: $_____
Steve Bava Collection

MARTINEZ
Face: XLCR
            SODA
           Star in shield
            WORKS
           MARTINEZ
Color: Aqua
Rarity:
Value: $_____
Steve Bava Collection

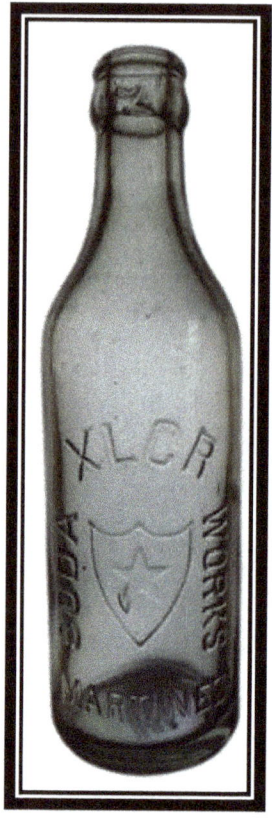 

MARYSVILLE
Face: B (Belden)
Color: Aqua
Rarity:
Value: $_____
Bob Voegtly Collection

MARYSVILLE
Face: B (Belden)
Color: Greenish
Rarity:
Value: $_____
Steve Bava Collection

MARYSVILLE
Bottom   B & M (Belden)
Color: Aqua
Rarity: Common
Value: $_____
Embossed on bottom
Steve & Christie Curtiss Collection

MARYSVILLE
Face: CAL. BOTTLING WKS.
         MARYSVILLE
Color: Aqua
Rarity: Scarce
Value: $_____
Steve & Christie Curtiss Collection

MARYSVILLE
Bottom: MARYSVILLE
        M. S. W.
        CAL.
Color: Sun Colored Amethyst
Rarity:
Value: $_____
Steve Bava Collection

MARYSVILLE
Face: YUBA
             BOTTLING WORKS
             MARYSVILLE, CAL.
Color: Aqua
Rarity:
Value: $_____
Steve Bava Collection

MAYFIELD (Palo Alto)
Face: MAYFIELD
           SODA WORKS
Color: Aqua
Rarity: Very Scarce
Value: $_____
Steve & Christie Curtiss Collection

MERCED

Face: BORELLO & ALLARIA
           TRADE B & A MARK
           MERCED CAL.

Color: Aqua
Rarity: Scarce
Value: $_____
Steve & Christie Curtiss Collection

MERCED

Face: F. A. L.
         MERCED

Color: Sun Colored Amethyst
Rarity:
Value: $_____
Steve Bava Collection

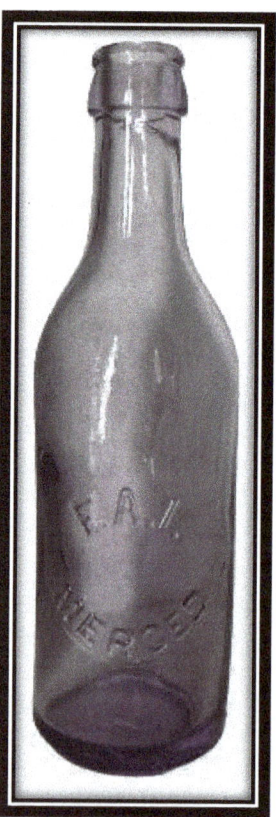

MODESTO

Face: CRYSTAL
            SODA WORKS
            MODESTO CAL.

Color: Aqua
Rarity: Rare
Value: $_____
Steve Bava Collection

MODESTO

Face: JACOBSEN & JORGENSEN
                Trade
              J & J
               Mark
            MODESTO
              CAL.

Color: Aqua
Rarity:
Value: $_____
Steve Bava Collection

MODESTO
Skirt: MODESTO
SODA WORKS

Color: Aqua
Rarity:
Value: $_____
Steve Bava Collection

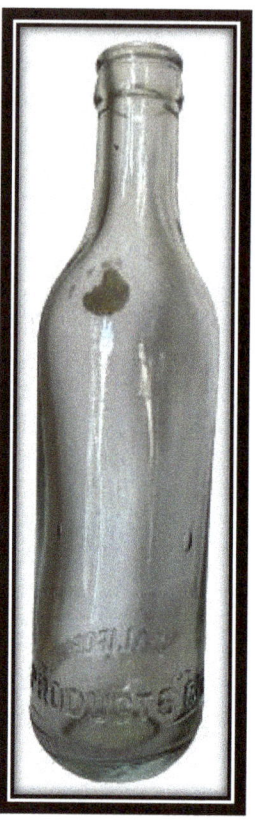

MOKELUMNE HILL (Circle)
Face: MOKELUMNE HILL
M. B.
SODA WORKS
Color: Aqua
Rarity: Very Scarce
Value: $_____
Steve Bava Collection

MOKELUMNE HILL (Circle)
Face: MOKELUMNE HILL
        SODA WORKS
Color: Aqua
Rarity: Scarce
Value: $_____
Steve & Christie Curtiss Collection

MONTEREY
Face: ENTERPRISE
         SODA WATER CO.
         MONTEREY
Base: NET CONTENTS 7½ OZ.
Color: Sun Colored Amethyst
Rarity: Common
Value: $_____
Steve Bava Collection

MONTEREY
Face: ENTERPRISE
          SODA WATER CO.
          MONTEREY
Base:
Color: Aqua
Rarity: Common
Value: $_____
John Burton Collection

MONTEREY
Face: ENTERPRISE
          SODA WATER CO.
          MONTEREY
Skirt: BOTTLE NEVER SOLD
Base:
Color: Aqua
Rarity: Common
Value: $_____
Marlon Christmann Collection

MONTEREY
Face: PROPERTY OF
         MONTEREY
         SODA WORKS
         CAL.
Color: Aqua
Rarity:
Value: $_____
Steve Bava Collection

MONTEREY
ENTERPRISE MONTEREY
Marlon Christmann Collection

NAPA
Face: ED. HENRY
          E.H.
          NAPA, CAL.
Color: Aqua
Rarity:
Value: $_____
Steve & Christie Curtiss Collection

NAPA
Face: ED. HENRY
            E.H.
            NAPA, CAL.
        NET CONTENTS 9 OZ.
Color: Aqua
Rarity:
Value: $_____
John Burton Collection

NAPA
Face: KNOX CRANATELI
              NAPA, CAL
Color: Aqua
Rarity: Common
Value: $_____
John Burton Collection

NAPA
Face: KNOX CRANATELI
              NAPA, Cal.
              NET CONTENTS 7 OZ.
Bottom: P. C. Co.
Color: Aqua
Rarity: Common
Value: $_____
John Burton Collection

NAPA
Face: KNOX CRANATELLI
             NAPA, CAL.
             NET CONTENTS 8 OZ.
Color: Aqua
Rarity: Common
Value: $_____
John Burton Collection

NAPA
Face: A. LUDWIG
             NAPA
             CAL.
Color: Aqua
Rarity: Scarce
Value: $_____
John Burton Collection

NAPA COUNTY
Face: P. SOMPS
          MINERAL WATER
          NAPA COUNTY
          CAL.
Color: Aqua
Rarity:
Value: $_____
Steve Bava Collection

NAPA COUNTY
Face: JACKSON
          NAPA
          SODA
Reverse: JACKSON'S
Color: Green
Rarity: Common
Value: $_____
Steve Bava Collection

NAPA COUNTY

Face: JACKSON'S
                  NAPA
                  SODA

Reverse: A NATURAL
           MINERAL WATER
           JACKSON'S
           THIS BOTTLE
           IS NEVER SOLD

Bottom: CONTENTS
           6 FLUID
           OUNCES

Color: Apple Green/ Aqua
Rarity: Common
Value: $_____
John Burton Collection

NAPA COUNTY (Vertical)

Face: JACKSON'S
              NAPA SODA
                 S.F.

Color: Amber
Rarity:
Value: $_____
John Burton Collection

NAPA COUNTY
Face: PHILLIPS'
                NAPA
            MINERAL WATER
Reverse: PHILLIPS'
                NAPA
            MINERAL WATER
Color: Aqua
Rarity:
Value: $_____
John Burton Collection

NAPA COUNTY
Face: PRIEST
                NAPA
Reverse: A NATURAL MINERAL
           WATER CARBONATED
              BOTTLED AT
             SAINT HELENA
                FROM
    THE PRIEST MINERAL SPRINGS
          NAPA, CO. CAL.
        NET CONTENTS 7 OZ.
Color: Aqua
Rarity:
Value: $_____
John Burton Collection

 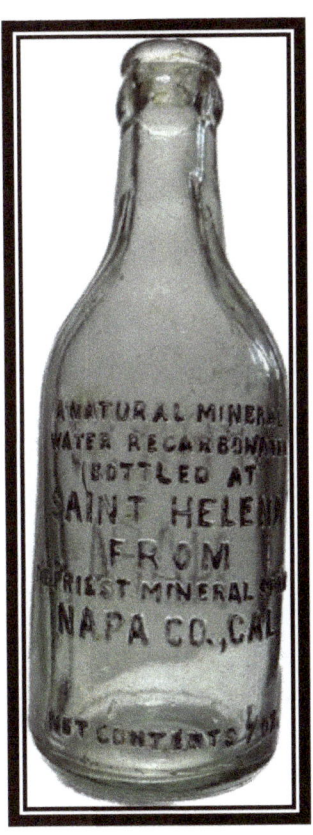

NAPA COUNTY
Face: PRIEST
                 NAPA
                 VALLEY
                 SODA
Reverse: NATURAL
              Priest image
            MINERAL WATER
Color: Aqua
Rarity:
Value: $_____
Steve Bava Collection

NAPA COUNTY
Face: SAMUEL
                 SODA
             TRADE M Mark
                 SPRINGS
Reverse: NATURAL
            MINERAL WATER
Color: Aqua
Rarity:
Value: $_____
John Burton Collection

NAPA COUNTY
Face: SAMUEL
SODA
TRADE M Mark
SPRINGS
Reverse: NATURAL
MINERAL WATER
Color: Amber
Rarity:
Value: $_____
John Burton Collection

NAPA COUNTY (Rounded Bottom)
Face: SAMUEL
SODA
BOTTLING
WORKS
ST. HELENA, CAL.
Color: Aqua
Rarity:
Value: $_____
John Burton Collection

NAPA COUNTY
Face: VICHY SPRINGS
              NAPA CO.
              CAL.

Reverse: NATURAL
              MINERAL WATER
              RFCARBONATED
Color: Aqua
Rarity:
Value: $_____
John Burton Collection

NAPA COUNTY
Face: NAPA ROCK
            MINERAL
            WATER
Color: Clear
Rarity: Extremely Common
Value $_____
John Burton Collection

NEVADA CITY
Face: RICHARD A. NOELL
              NEVADA CITY
              SODA WORKS
Base: NET CONTENTS 8 OZ.
Color: Aqua
Rarity: Extremely Common
Value $_____
Gary Christensen Collection

NEVADA CITY
Face: RICHARD A. NOELL
              NEVADA CITY
              SODA WORKS
Base: NET CONTENTS 8 OZ.
Color: Aqua, Clear & Green
Rarity: Extremely Common
Value $_____
Steve & Christie Curtiss Collection

NEVADA CITY
Face: JOHN FINN
         SODA WORKS
Color: Aqua
Rarity:
Value: $_____
Image

NEVADA CITY
Face: E. T. R. POWELL
        NEVADA CITY
        SODA WORKS
Base: NET CONTENTS
        7 FLUID OUNCES
Color: Clear
Rarity:
Value: $_____
John Burton Collection

NEVADA CITY

Face: NEVADA CITY
          SODA WORKS
          E. T. POWELL

Color: Aqua

Rarity:

Value: $_____

Steve Bava Collection

NEWMAN

Face: NEWMAN
          SODA WORKS
          H. MEIER
          NEWMAN, CAL.

Color: Aqua

Rarity:

Value: $_____

Mike Ertmoed Collection

OAKDALE
Face: J & J
           OAKDALE
Color: Aqua
Rarity: Very Rare
Value: $_____
Steve Bava Collection

OAKDALE
Face: OAKDALE SODA WORKS OAKDALE, CAL.
Color: Aqua
Rarity:
Value: $_____
Steve & Christie Curtiss Collection

OAKDALE

Face: OAKDALE SODA WORKS OAKDALE CAL.
                CONTENTS 7 OZ.

Color: Aqua
Rarity:
Value: $_____
Steve & Christie Curtiss Collection

OAKDALE

Face: PETER JORGENSEN
                TRADE
                P. J.
                MARK
                OAKDALE
                CAL.

Color: Clear
Rarity:
Value: $_____
Steve & Christie Curtiss Collection

OAKDALE
Face: PETER JORGENSEN
TRADE
P. J.
MARK
OAKDALE
CAL.
Color: Sun Colored Amethyst
Rarity:
Value: $_____
Steve Bava Collection

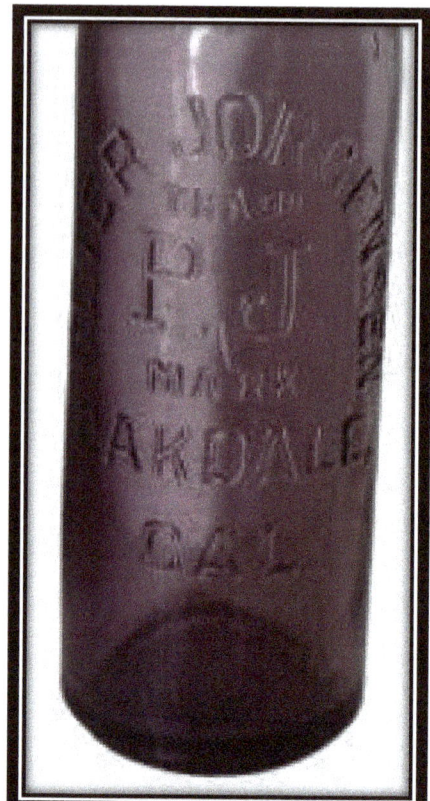

OAKLAND
ALAMEDA
Hands Clasping
SODA WATER CO.
OAKLAND, CAL.
BOTTLE NEVER SOLD
Color: Aqua
Rarity:
Value $_____
Steve & Christie Curtiss Collection

OAKLAND

ALAMEDA SODA WATER CO
(Vertical Embossing)
Hands Clasping
REG'D
OAKLAND, CAL.

Color: Aqua
Rarity: Rare
Value $_____
Steve Bava Collection

OAKLAND
Skirt: ALAMEDA
Hands Clasping
SODA WATER CO.

Color: Aqua
Rarity:
Value: $_____
Steve & Christie Curtiss Collection

 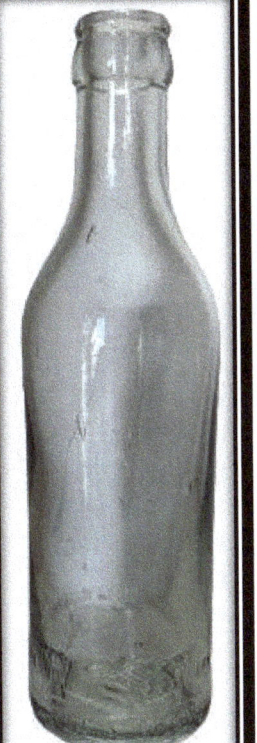  

OAKLAND
Skirt: ALAMEDA SODA WATER CO.
              OAKLAND, CAL.
              Hands Clasping
Color: Aqua
Rarity:
Value: $_____
Steve & Christie Curtiss Collection

OAKLAND
Face: IMPERAL
              GINGER ALE
                 AND
              SODA WATER CO.
                OAKLAND
                  CAL.
Color: Aqua
Rarity:
Value: $_____
John Burton Collection

OAKLAND
Face: IMPERAL
            GINGER ALE
            AND
            SODA WATER CO.
            OAKLAND
            CAL.
Color: Clear
Rarity:
Value: $_____
Steve Bava Collection

OAKLAND
Face: IMPERAL
            GINGER ALE
            AND
            SODA WATER CO.
            OAKLAND
            CAL.
Color: Green
Rarity:
Value: $_____
Color: Aqua
Rarity:
Value: $_____
Steve Bava Collection

OAKLAND (Vertical Embossing)
Face: HIGHLAND
GINGER ALE
REG'D
OAKLAND, CAL.
Color: Aqua
Rarity: Very Rare
Value: $_____
Steve Bava Collection

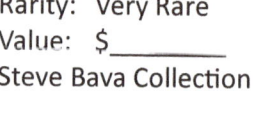

OAKLAND (Vertical Embossing
Face: HIGHLAND
GINGER ALE
(Without REG'D)
OAKLAND, CAL.
Color: Aqua
Rarity: Very Rare
Value: $_____
Steve Bava Collection

OAKLAND
Face: HIGHLAND
          MINERAL
          WATER
Reverse: A
          NATURAL
          MINERAL
          WATER
          Logo
Color: Aqua
Rarity: Common
Value: $_____
Steve & Christie Curtiss Collection

OAKLAND
Face: O.P.S.W. CO.
          Bottle
          TRADE MARK
          OAKLAND, CAL.
Color: Aqua
Rarity:
Value: $_____
Steve Bava Collection

OAKLAND
Face: OAKLAND
        <rays> INC.
        STEAM SODA WORKS
        BOTTLE IS NOT SOLD
Color: Aqua
Rarity:
Value: $_____
Steve & Christie Curtiss Collection

OAKLAND
Face: OAKLAND PIONEER
        <Bottle> TRADE MARK
        SODA WATER CO.
        THIS BOTTLE IS NEVER SOLD
Color: Aqua
Rarity:
Value: $_____
Steve Bava Collection

OAKLAND

Face: OAKLAND PIONEER
TRADE <Bottle> MARK
SODA WATER CO.
THIS BOTTLE IS NEVER SOLD

Color: Clear

Rarity:

Value: $_____

Steve Bava Collection

OAKLAND

Face: OAKLAND PIONEER
TRADE <Bottle> MARK
SODA WATER CO.
THIS BOTTLE IS NEVER SOLD

Color: Aqua

Rarity:

Value: $_____

Steve & Christie Curtiss Collection

OAKLAND
Face: OAKLAND PIONEER
         TRADE <Bottle> MARK
         SODA WATER CO.
         THIS BOTTLE IS NEVER SOLD
Color: Purple
Rarity:
Value: $_____
Bob Voegtly Collection

OAKLAND
Face: OAKLAND
         HONEE
         BEVERAGE
Color: Clear
Rarity:
Value: $_____
John Burton Collection

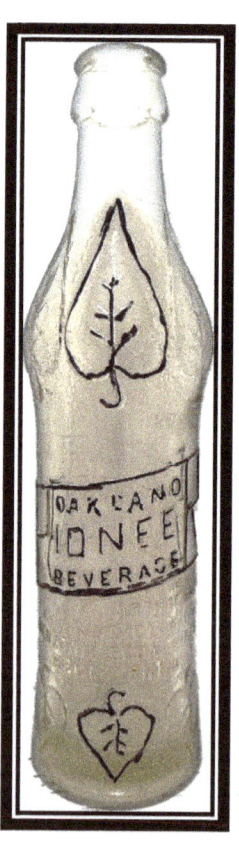

ONTARIO

Face: O. K.
                BOTTLING WORKS
                NET CONTENTS
                8 FL. OZ.
                ONTARIO, CAL.
                THIS BOTTLE
                MUST BE RETURNED

Color: Aqua
Rarity:
Value: $_____
Steve & Christie Curtiss Collection

ONTARIO

Face: O. K.
                BOTTLING WORKS
                ONTARIO, CAL.
                THIS BOTTLE
                MUST BE RETURNED

Color: Aqua
Rarity:
Value: $_____
Steve & Christie Curtiss Collection

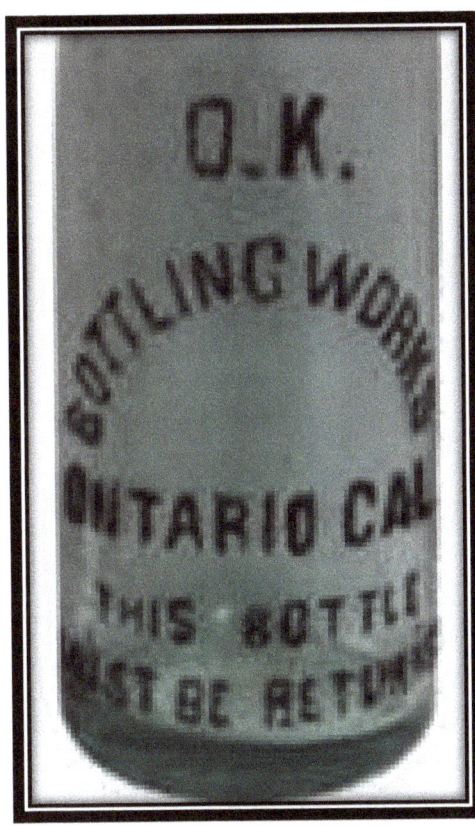

OROVILLE
Bottom: O. S. W.
                OROVILLE
Color: Aqua
Rarity:
Value: $_____
Steve Bava Collection

OXNARD
Bottom: OXNARD
                SODA WORKS
                OXNARD
                    CAL.
Color: Aqua
Rarity:
Value: $_____
Steve Bava Collection

OXNARD

Skirt: OXNARD SODA WORKS
            OXNARD CAL.

Color: Clear
Rarity:
Value: $_____
Steve & Christie Curtiss Collection

PACIFIC GROVE

Face: PACIFIC GROVE
         SODA WORKS

Color: Aqua
Rarity:
Value: $_____
Bob Voegtly Collection

PALO ALTO
Face: PALO ALTO
          SODA WORKS
Color: Aqua
Rarity:
Value: $_____
Steve & Christie Curtiss Collection

PASADENA
Face: COLES
          ENGLISH
          GINGER-ALE
          CE CE
     BOTTLED & GUARANTEED
          BY
    PENINSULAR MFG. CO.
          PASADENA
          CAL.
Color: Aqua
Rarity:
Value: $_____
Steve Bava Collection

PASADENA
Face: CROWN CITY
          BOTTLING CO.
          PASADENA, CAL.
Color: Clear
Rarity: Scarce
Value: $_____
Marlon Christmann Collection

PASADENA
Skirt: LIVITI DISTILLED WATER CO.
            PASADENA, CAL.
Color: Aqua
Rarity:
Value: $_____
Steve & Christie Curtiss Collection

PASADENA
Face: MT. LOWE
            CARBONATING
            AND
            DISTILLING WORKS
            PASADENA,
            CAL.

Color: Aqua
Rarity: Extremely Rare
Value: $_____
Bob Hirsch Collection

PASO ROBLES
Face: PASO ROBLES SODA
          T. BROOKS
          P. R.
Color: Aqua
Rarity:
Value: $_____
Steve Bava Collection

PETALUMA
Face: PETALUMA SODA
               AND
               SELTZER WORKS
Bottom: PET
Color: Aqua
Rarity: Scarce
Value: $_____
John Burton Collection

PETALUMA
Face: PETALUMA SODA
               AND
               SELTZER WORKS
               E. KLAMMER
Bottom: PET
Color: Aqua
Rarity: Scarce
Value: $_____
John Burton Collection

Also comes with *E. Klammer* slugged out

119

PETALUMA
Face: KLAMMER & MALZ
         TRADE PET MARK
         PETALUMA
         CAL.
Color: Aqua
Rarity: Scarce
Value: $_____
John Burton Collection

PETALUMA
Face: KLAMMER & MALZ
         TRADE PET MARK
         PETALUMA
         AND
         SAN RAFAEL
Color: Aqua
Rarity: Extremely Rare
Value: $_____
Steve Bava Collection

PETALUMA
Face: WHISTLE
              REGISTERED
              PAT. NO. 70843, 1926
Reverse: WHISTLE
              6 ½ FLD. OZS.
              REG. U.S.
Bottom: PETALUMA, CAL.
John Burton Collection

PITTSBURG
Face: PITTSBURG
           SODA WORKS
           PITTSBURG, CAL.
Color: Aqua
Rarity:
Value: $_____
Steve & Christie Curtiss Collection

PITTSBURG
Face: BLACK DIAMOND SODA WORKS
          R.A. DIMAGGIO
Color:
Rarity: Extremely Rare
Value: $_____
Steve Bava Collection

PLACERVILLE
Face: SCHERRER BROS.
          PLACEVILLE
          CONTENTS 7 OZ.
Color: Clear
Rarity:
Value: $_____
Steve & Christie Curtiss Collection

PLACERVILLE
Face: SHERRER BROS.
PLACERVILLE
Color: Aqua
Rarity:
Value: $_____
Steve & Christie Curtiss Collection

SCHERRER misspelt

PLACERVILLE
Face: R. A. HOOK
SUCCESSOR TO
SCHERRER BROS.
PLACERVILLE
Color: Clear
Rarity: Extremely Rare
Value: $_____
Steve & Christie Curtiss Collection

PLEASENTON

Face: DERBY'S

          Trade Mark

          FINE DRINKS

          PLEASENTON, CAL.

Color: Aqua

Rarity: Extremely Rare

Value; $_____

Steve Bava Collection

POMONA

Face: POMONA SODA WORKS

          POMONA

              CAL.

Color: Clear

Rarity:

Value: $_____

Letters go below CAL

Steve & Christie Curtiss Collection

POMONA

Face: POMONA SODA WORKS
              POMONA
                    CAL.

Color: Aqua
Rarity:
Value: $_____
Letters go below CAL
Steve Bava Collection

POMONA

Face: POMONA SODA WORKS
              POMONA
                    CAL.

Color: Aqua
Rarity:
Value: $_____
Letters stop above CAL
Steve & Christie Curtiss Collection

POMONA

Face: REGISTERED
        MILNER'S BOTTLING WORKS
        POMONA,
        CAL.

Color: Light Green
Rarity:
Value: $_____
Steve & Christie Curtiss Collection

POMONA

Face: O. K.
        BOTTLING WORKS
        POMONA, CAL.
        THIS BOTTLE
        IS NOT TO BE SOLD

Color: Aqua
Rarity:
Value: $_____
Steve Bava Collection

POPE VALLEY (Napa County)
Face: POPE MINERAL WATER
           P. GUILLAUME
           PROP.
           NAPA, CAL.

Color: Aqua
Rarity: Extremely Rare
Value: $_____
Steve Bava Collection

POPE VALLEY (Napa County)
Face: P. GUILLAUME
           MINERAL WATER
           POPE VALLEY
           NAPA, CO.
           CAL.

Color: Aqua
Rarity: Extremely Rare
Value: $_____
John Burton Collection

PORTERVILLE (Circle)
Face: PORTERVILLE
          SODA
          WORKS
Color: Clear
Rarity:
Steve & Christie Curtiss Collection

PORTERVILLE (Circle)
Face: PORTERVILLE
          SODA
          WORKS
Color: Aqua
Rarity:
Steve Bava Collection

PORTERVILLE (Circle)
Face: PORTERVILLE
           SODA
          WORKS
     PORTERVILLE, CAL.
Color: Aqua
Rarity:
Value: $_____
Steve Bava Collection

PORTERVILLE
Face: RICHARDSON'S
        BOTTLING WKS.
         PORTERVILLE
Color: Clear
Rarity:
Value: $_____
Marlon Christmann Collection

PRESTON
Face: BARCAL
             MINERAL WATER
Color: Aqua
Rarity: Semi Common
Value: $_____
John Burton Collection

 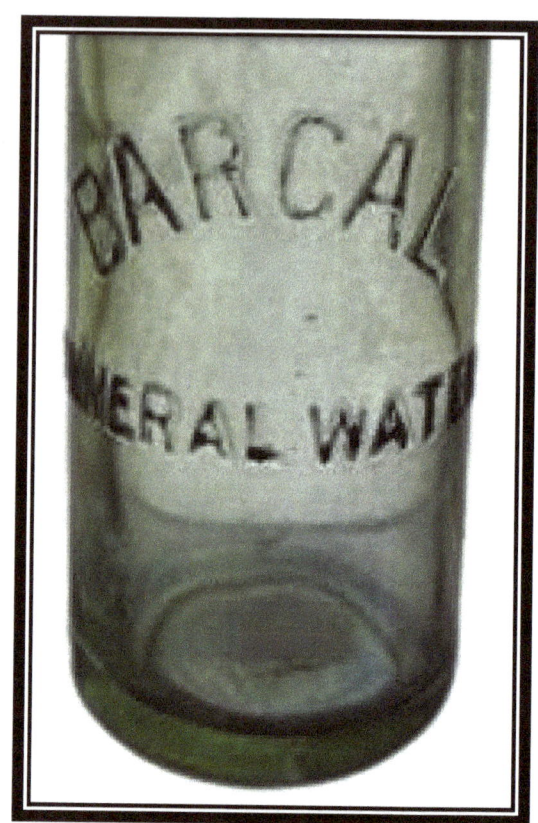

PRESTON
Face: LONGFELLOW
Reverse: LONGFELLOW
Color: Clear
Rarity: Extremely Common
Value: $_____
John Burton Collection

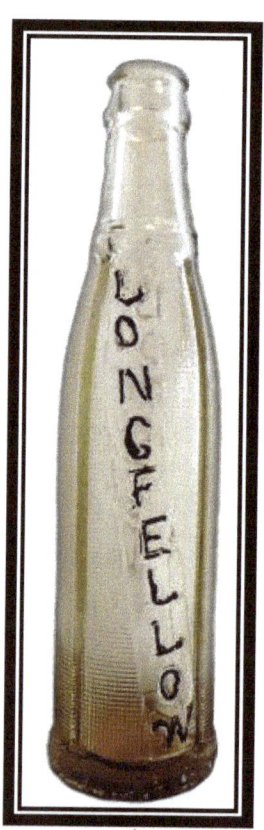 

PRESTON
Face: LONGFELLOW
Reverse: BARCAL
                JOHN
                KOLLING
                PRESTON,
                CAL.

Color: Clear
Rarity: Extremely Common
Value: $_____
John Burton Collection

RED BLUFF
Face: CONE
                I. & C. S. CO.
                R.B.
Color: Aqua & Clear
Rarity:
Value $_____
Steve & Christie Curtiss Collection

131

RED BLUFF (Variant)
Face: CONE
          I. & R. CO.
          R.B.
Color: Clear & Sun Colored Amethyst
Rarity: Common
Value $_____
Steve & Christie Curtiss Collection

RED BLUFF
Face: G. M. W.
          R. B.
Color: Aqua
Rarity:
Value: $_____
Steve Bava Collection

REDDING

Face: JOS. HOEFER
             SODA WORKS
              REDDING

Color: Aqua

Rarity:

Value $_____

Steve & Christie Curtiss Collection

REDDING

Face: ZEIS & SONS CO.
              REDDING CAL.
     THIS BOTTLE IS NEVER SOLD

Color: Aqua

Rarity:

Value: $_____

John Burton Collection

REDDING

Face: ZEIS & SONS CO.
            REDDING CAL.

Color: Aqua

Rarity:

Value: $_____

Steve & Christie Curtiss Collection

REDLANDS

Face: REDLANDS BOTTLING
            WORKS
            J. T. ALLEN PROP.

Color: Aqua

Rarity:

Value: $_____

Marlon Christmann Collection

REDWOOD CITY

Face: REDWOOD CITY SODA WATER CO.
REDWOOD, CITY

Color: Aqua
Rarity:
Value: $_____
Steve Bava Collection

REDWOOD CITY

Face: HEANEY BROS.
REDWOOD CITY, CAL.

Color: Aqua
Rarity:
Value: $_____
Marlon Christmann Collection

REDWOOD CITY
Face: HIGHLAND
           GINGER ALE CO.
           REDWOOD CITY, CAL.
Color: Aqua
Rarity: Very Rare
Value: $_____
Steve & Christie Curtiss Collection

REDWOOD CITY
Face: YOSEMITE
       SODA WORKS
       REDWOOD CITY
Color: Extremely Rare
Rarity:
Value: $_____
Steve Bava Collection

RICHMOND In Circle
Face: RICHMOND SODA WORKS
                RSW
             RICHMOND

Color: Aqua
Rarity:
Value: $_____
Steve & Christie Curtiss Collection

RICHMOND
Face: RICHMOND SODA WORKS
                RSW
          POINT RICHMOND

Color: Aqua
Rarity:
Value: $_____
John Burton Collection

RICHMOND
Face: RICHMOND SODA WORKS
                RSW
            POINT RICHMOND
Color: Aqua
Rarity:
Value: $_____
Steve & Christie Curtiss Collection

RIVERSIDE (Skirt Embossed)
Skirt: RIVERSIDE SODA WORKS
            RIVERSIDE, CA.
Color: Aqua
Rarity:
Value: $_____
Steve & Christie Curtiss Collection

RIVERSIDE (Skirt Embossed)
Skirt: RIVERSIDE SODA WORKS
              RIVERSIDE, CA.
Color: Yellowish Green
Rarity:
Value: $_____
Steve & Christie Curtiss Collection

RIVERSIDE
Face: O. K. BOTTLING Co.
              RIVERSIDE
Color: Aqua
Rarity:
Value: $_____
Steve Bava Collection

ROSEVILLE

Face: ROSEVILLE
             SODA WATER BOTTLING
             WORKS
             NET CONTENTS 8 OZS.

Color: Clear
Rarity: Rare
Value: $_____
Steve & Christie Curtiss Collection

ROSEVILLE

Face: ROSEVILLE
             SODA WATER BOTTLING
             WORKS
             CONTENTS 8 OZS.

Color: Clear
Rarity: Rare
Value: $_____
Steve & Christie Curtiss Collection

SACRAMENTO
Face: ARISTO
          MINERAL WATER
          AND
          SIPHON CO.
          SACRAMENTO
          CAL.
Color: Aqua
Rarity: Scarce
Value: $_____
Steve & Christie Curtiss Collection

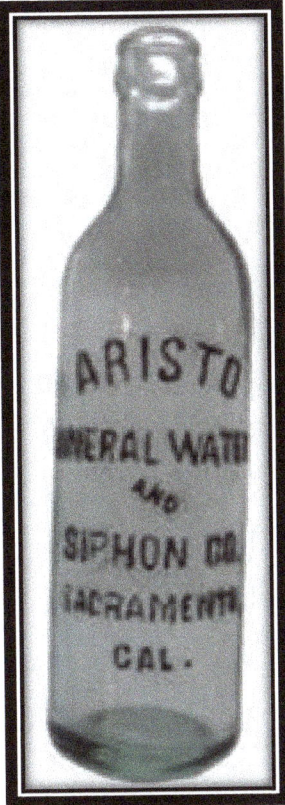

SACRAMENTO
Face: ARISTO
Color: Aqua
Rarity: Scarce
Value: $_____
Steve Bava Collection

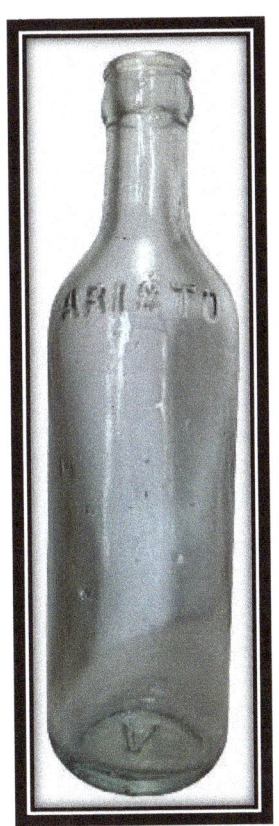

SACRAMENTO
Skirt: ARISTO
           SACRAMENTO
Color: Aqua
Rarity: Common
Value: $_____
Steve & Christie Curtiss Collection

SACRAMENTO
Face: C. SCHNERR & CO.
           SACRAMENTO
           CAL.
           TRADE MARK REGISTERED
           BOTTLE IS NEVER SOLD
Base: CAPITOL SODA
           WORKS
Color: Aqua
Rarity:
Value: $_____
Marlon Christmann Collection

SACRAMENTO
Face: C. SCHNERR & CO.
           SACRAMENTO
              CAL.
      TRADE MARK REGISTERED
      BOTTLE IS NEVER SOLD

Color: Aqua
Rarity:
Value: $_____
Steve Bava Collection

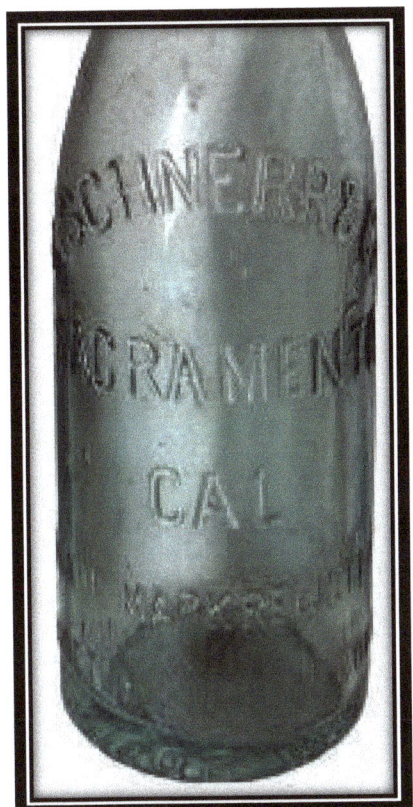

SACRAMENTO
Face: C. SCHNERR & CO.
           SACRAMENTO
              CAL.
      TRADE MARK REGISTERED
      BOTTLE IS NEVER SOLD

Color: Light Purple
Rarity:
Value: $_____
Steve Bava Collection

SACRAMENTO
Skirt: **SCHNERR**
          SAC-CAL
Color: Light Purple
Rarity:
Value: $_____
Steve & Christie Curtiss Collection

SACRAMENTO
Face: SILVER GATE
        SCHNEPP
        BROS.
        SODA WORKS
Color: Aqua
Rarity:
Value: $_____
Marlon Christmann Collection

SACRAMENTO

Face: CALIFORNIA
BOTTLING WORKS
T. BLAUTH
407 K STREET
SACRAMENTO

Color: Aqua
Rarity:
Value: $_____
Steve Bava Collection

SACRAMENTO

Face: CALIFORNIA
BOTTLING WORKS
THEO BLAUTH SONS CO.
407 K STREET
SACRAMENTO

Color: Aqua
Rarity: Scarce
Value: $_____
Steve Bava Collection

SACRAMENTO
Face: GROSJEAN & HOLDAWAY
            Monogram
            SACRAMENTO
                CAL.
Reverse: Blank
Color: Aqua
Rarity: Very Scarce
Value: $_____
Steve & Christie Curtiss Collection

SACRAMENTO
Face: GROSJEAN & HOLDAWAY
            Monogram
            SACRAMENTO
                CAL.
Reverse: COCA COLA
Color: Aqua
Rarity: Very Scarce
Value: $_____
IMage

SACRAMENTO
Face: S. C. O. N. M. W. ASSN.
         SACRAMENTO, CAL.
Color: Aqua
Rarity: Common
Value: $_____
John Burton Collection

SACRAMENTO
Face: THIS BOTTLE
         IS THE PROPERTY OF
            LEWIS DELEW
               BOTTLER
         SACRAMENTO, CAL.
Color: Sun Colored Amethyst
Rarity:
Value: $_____
Steve Bava Collection

SACRAMENTO
Face: THIS BOTTLE
          IS THE PROPERTY OF
          LEWIS DELEW
          BOTTLER
          SACRAMENTO, CAL.
Color: Clear
Rarity:
Value: $_____
Steve Bava Collection

SACRAMENTO
Face: THIS BOTTLE
          IS THE PROPERTY OF
          LEWIS DELEW
          BOTTLER
          SACRAMENTO, CAL.
Color: Light Purple
Rarity:
Value: $_____
Steve Bava Collection

SACRAMENTO

Face: SUN-RISE-SODA-WORKS
                     Logo
               SACRAMENTO, CAL.

Reverse: NET. CONTENTS 8 OZ.

Color: Aqua

Rarity:

Value: $_____

Steve Bava collection

SACRAMENTO

Face: SUN-RISE-SODA-WORKS
                     Logo
               SACRAMENTO, CAL.

Color: Aqua

Rarity:

Value: $_____

Steve & Christie Curtiss Collection

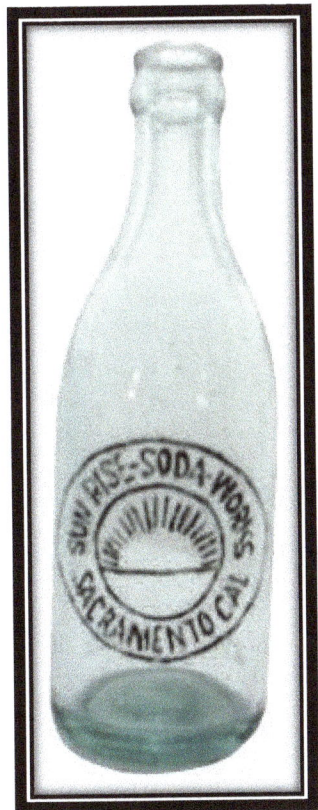 

SACRAMENTO
Face: THE GEO. WAIT
           CARBONATING
               CO.
           SACRAMENTO, CAL.
Color: Sun Colored Amethyst
Rarity:
Value: $_____
Steve & Christie Curtiss Collection

SACRAMENTO (Circle)
Face: WHITE STAR SODA WKS
             ★
          SACRAMENTO
Color: Clear
Rarity:
Value: $_____
Steve & Christie Curtiss Collection

SACRAMENTO
Face: WILSON HALL & CO.
            SACRAMENTO
                CAL.
        BOTTLE NOT SOLD
Color: Aqua
Rarity:
Value: $_____
Image

SACRAMENTO
Face: WILSON MF'G CO.
            HIGH GRADE
        CARBONATED DRINK
        SACRAMENTO, CAL.
        ABOVE TRADE MARK
            PROTECTED
Color: Aqua
Rarity:
Value: $_____
Steve & Christie Curtiss Collection

 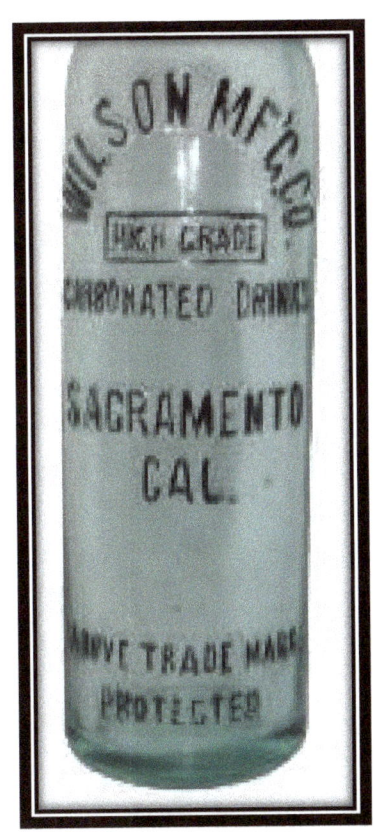

SACRAMENTO
Face: BOTTLE NOT SOLD
          WILSON MFG. CO.
          W. M. CO.
          SACRAMENTO
Color: Aqua
Rarity:
Value: $_____
Steve Bava Collection

SACRAMENTO
Face: WILSON MFG. CO.
         SACRAMENTO, CAL.
         Bottle Not to be Sold
Color: Aqua
Rarity:
Value: $_____
Steve & Christie Curtiss Collection

SALINAS
Face: SALINAS
              SODA WORKS
              SALINAS, CAL.
Color: Clear
Rarity:
Value: $_____
Steve & Christie Curtiss Collection

SALINAS
Face: SALINAS SODA WORKS
              P. STEIGELMAN
              SALINAS, CAL.
              BOTTLE NEVER SOLD
Color: Aqua
Rarity:
Value: $_____
Steve Bava Collection

SALINAS
Face: SALINAS SODA WORKS
          P. STEIGELMAN
          SALINAS, CAL.
          BOTTLE NEVER SOLD
Color: Apple Green
Rarity:
Value: $_____
Steve Bava Collection

SALINAS
Face: PARAISO MINERAL WATER
          BOTTLED BY
          P. STEIGELMAN
          SALINAS, CAL.
Color: Aqua
Rarity:
Value: $_____
Steve Bava Collection

SALINAS
Face: SALINAS BOTTLING WORKS
            B & M
            SALINAS
            CAL.
Color: Apple Green
Rarity:
Value: $_____
Steve Bava Collection

SALINAS
Face: SALINAS BOTTLING WORKS
            B & M
            SALINAS
            CAL.
Color: Aqua
Rarity:
Value: $_____
Steve & Christie Curtiss Collection

SAUSALITO
Face: MASON & CO.
         SAUSALITO, CAL.
Color: Aqua
Rarity: Very Scarce
Value: $_____
John Burton Collection

SAUSALITO (Vertical Embossing)
Face: MASON
         SODA WORKS
         SAUSALITO
Color: Aqua
Rarity: Very Rare
Value: $_____
John Burton Collection

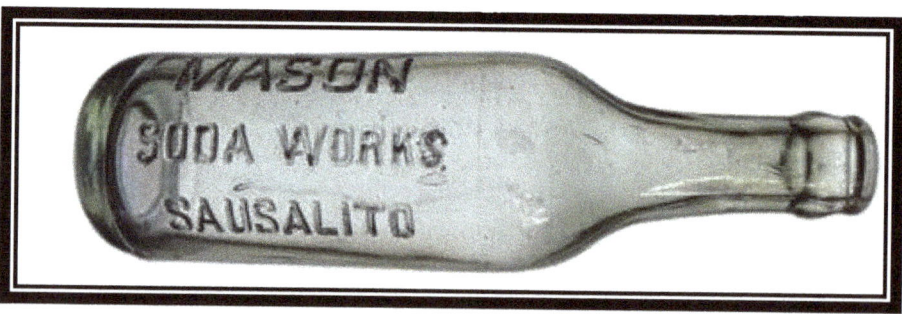 

SAUSALITO (Vertical Embossing)
Face: MASON
        SODA WORKS
         SAUSALITO
Color: Light Purple
Rarity: Very Rare
Value: $_____
Steve Bava Collection

SAUSALITO
Face: MASON
        SAUSALITO
        GINGERALE
Color: Aqua
Rarity: Very rare
Value: $_____
Dan Brown collection

SAUSALITO
Face: WHISTLE
               REGISTERED
               PAT. NO. 70843, 1926
Reverse: WHISTLE
               6 ½ FLD. OZS.
               REG. U.S.
Bottom: SAUSALITO
               CAL.
John Burton Collection

SAUSALITO
Face: DRINK
               MASON's
               SODA
               IT'S GOOD
Reverse: RETURN TO
               MASON & CO.
               SAUSALITO, CAL.
Color: Aqua
Rarity: Scarce
Value: $_____
John Burton Collection

SAUSALITO
Face: *Meyers*
Color: Aqua
Rarity:
Value: $_____
John Burton Collection

 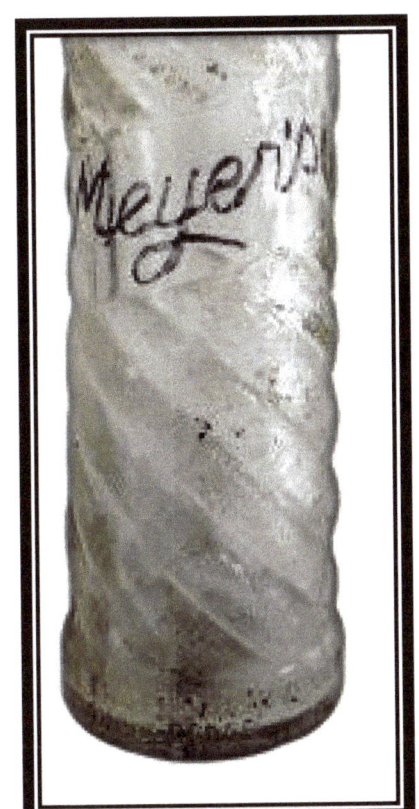

SAUSALITO
Face: *Meyers SPECIAL*
Skirt: CONTENTS 10 FLD. OZS.
Color: Aqua
Rarity:
Value: $_____
John Burton Collection

SAUSALITO
Face: B & H
Bettencourt & Hogan
Color: Aqua
Rarity: Semi Common
Value $_____)_
Bob Voegtly Collection

SAN ANSELMO
Face: SAN ANSELMO
            BOTTLING
                CO.
            SAN RAFAEL, CAL.
Color: Aqua
Rarity: Scarce
Value: $_____
John Burton Collection

SAN ANSELMO
Face: SAN ANSELMO
          BOTTLING
              CO.
          SAN RAFAEL
              CAL.
Color: Aqua
Rarity:
Value: $_____
John Burton Collection

SAN BERNARDINO
Face: EXCELSIOR BOTTLING
             WORKS
          SAN BERNADINO
Color:
Rarity:
Value: $_____
Bruce Silva Collection

SAN BERNARDINO
Face: SAN BERNARDINO
           S. & S.
        EAGLE SODA WORKS
Color: Aqua
Rarity:
Value: $_____

SAN BERNARDINO (Embossed on Skirt)
Skirt: SAN BERNARDINO SODA WORKS
Color: Aqua
Rarity:
Value: $_____
Marlon Christmann Collection

SAN DIEGO
Face: EXCELSIOR
            BOTTLING WORKS
               SAN DIEGO
                   CAL.

Color: Aqua
Rarity:
Value: $_____
Steve Bava Collection

SAN DIEGO
Face: MONARCH SODA WORKS
                Lion image
              A. HAYDIS & SON
                 SAN DIEGO,
                     CAL.

Color: Aqua
Rarity: Extremely Rare
Value: $_____
Image

SAN DIEGO
Face: SAN DIEGO
           TRADE ★ MARK
           SODA WORKS
Color: Apple Green
Rarity:
Value: $_____

SAN DIEGO
Face: SAN DIEGO
           TRADE ★ MARK
           SODA WORKS
Color: Aqua
Rarity:
Value: $_____
Steve & Christie Curtiss Collection

SAN DIEGO
Face   THE
        DISTILLED WATER
            AND
        BOTTLING CO.
        SAN DIEGO,
            CALIF.
Color: Aqua
Rarity:
Value: $_____
Image

SAN DIEGO
Face: SILVER GATE
        SCHNEPP
            BROS.
        SODA WORKS
Color: Aqua
Rarity:
Value: $_____
Steve Bava Collection

SAN DIEGO
Face: BRADLEY
              SPRING WATER
              (Eagle)
             SAN DIEGO, CAL.
Color: Apple Green
Rarity: Very Rare
Value: $_____
Rick Hall Collection

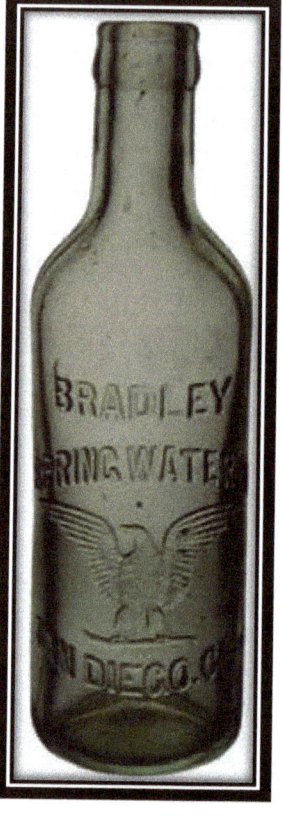 

SAN DIEGO
Face: Blank
Bottom: Rex
         Bottling Co.
         San Diego
Color: Aqua
Rarity:
Value: $_____
Steve & Christie Curtis Collection

SAN FRANCISCO
Face: ALTA BOTTLING CO.
        22ND AVE. & T ST.
        SAN FRANCISCO
Color: Aqua
Rarity:
Value: $_____
Steve Bava Collection

SAN FRANCISCO
Face: AMERICAN
              (Flag)
        MINERAL WATER CO.
              S.F.
Color: Aqua
Rarity: Scarce
Value $_____
Steve Bava Collection
(Stubby Bottle)

SAN FRANCISCO
Face: AMERICAN
          (Flag)
       SODA WORKS
         S.F.
Color: Aqua
Rarity: Scarce
Value $_____
Steve Bava Collection

SAN FRANCISCO
Face: BAY CITY SODA WATER CO.
         SAN FRANCISCO
           CAL.
         REGISTERED
Color: Aqua
Rarity: Very Scarce
Value: $_____
Steve Bava Collection

 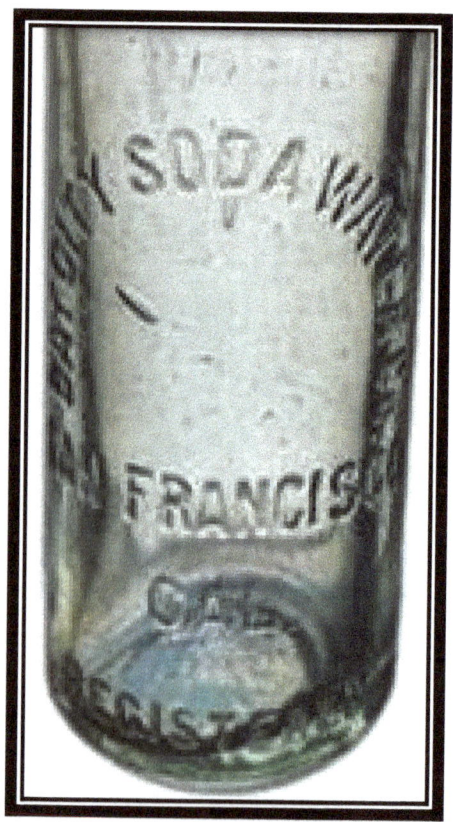

SAN FRANCISCO
Face: BAY CITY SODA WATER CO.
                SAN FRANCISCO
                        CAL.
                REGISTERED

Color: Aqua
Rarity: Very Scarce
Value: $_____
Steve & Christie Curtiss Collection

SAN FRANCISCO
Face: BELFAST
            Trade /B \Mark
            GINGER ALE
                    S.F.

Color: Aqua
Rarity: Semi Common
Value: $_____
John Burton Collection

SAN FRANCISCO
Face: /B \
          BELFAST
          7 FL. OZ.
Color: Clear
Rarity: Scarce
Value: $_____
John Burton Collection

SAN FRANCISCO
Face: CALIFORNIA
          PURE WATER CO.
             (Logo)
          SAN FRANCISCO
Color: Light Green
Rarity: Very Scarce
Value: $_____
Steve Bava Collection

SAN FRANCISCO
Face: CALIFORNIA
            PURE WATER CO.
            (Logo)
            SAN FRANCISCO
Color: Amber
Rarity: Very Scarce
Value: $_____
Steve Bava Collection

SAN FRANCISCO
Face: CROWN

J.J. BLIVEN & CO.
SODA WATER
COMPANY
SAN FRANCISCO, CAL.
Color: Clear
Rarity:
Value: $_____
Steve Bava Collection

SAN FRANCISCO
Face:
SODA WORKS
Color: Aqua
Rarity:
Value: $_____
Steve & Christie Curtiss Collection

SAN FRANCISCO
Face:
SODA WORKS
Color: Aqua
Rarity:
Value: $_____
Steve Bava Collection

SAN FRANCISCO
Face: CROWN
           SODA WATER CO.
           S. F.
Color: Aqua
Rarity:
Value: $_____
Steve & Christie Curtiss Collection

SAN FRANCISCO
Face: CROWN
           SODA WATER CO.
           S. F.
           JAS. I. BLIVEN & CO.
Color: Aqua
Rarity: Very Scarce
Value: $_____
Bob Voegtly Collection

SAN FRANCISCO
Face: CLUB
                     SODA
Reverse: MADE FROM
                NATURAL MINERAL
                     WATER
                Re-Carbonated
Base: ENTERPRISE PIONEER BOTTLING CO.
                SAN FRANCISCO

Color: Aqua
Rarity:
Value: $_____
Steve Bava Collection

CLUB SODA REVERSE

SAN FRANCISCO
Face: EGGERS & CO.
        FINE BEVERAGES
          S. F. CAL.
Color: Aqua
Rarity: Rare
Value: $_____
Image

SAN FRANCISCO
Face: ENTERPRISE
        SODA WORKS
          S. F.
Color: Aqua
Rarity: Common
Value: $_____
Steve Bava Collection

SAN FRANCISCO
Face: ENTERPRISE SODA WORKS
            SAN FRANCISCO
Color: Aqua
Rarity: Scarce
Value: $_____
IMAGE

SAN FRANCISCO
Face: EUREKA-CALIFORNIA

            SODA WATER CO.
                    S.F.
Color: Clear
Rarity:
Value: $_____
Steve Bava Collection

SAN FRANCISCO
Face: EUREKA-CALIFORNIA

SODA WATER CO.
            S.F.
Bottom   E-C
Color: Aqua
Rarity: Rare
Value: $_____
John Burton Collection

SAN FRANCISCO
Face: EUREKA-CALIFORNIA

SODA WATER CO.
            S.F.
Color: Amber
Rarity:
Value: $_____
Image

SAN FRANCISCO
Face: GOLDEN WEST
             SODA WORKS
             SAN FRANCISCO
             CAL.
Bottom: Horseshoe
Color: Aqua
Rarity: Very Scarce
Value: $_____
John Burton Collection

SAN FRANCISCO
Face: GOLDEN WEST
             SODA WORKS
             SAN FRANCISCO,
             CAL.
Bottom: Horseshoe
Color: Yellowish Green
Rarity: Very Scarce
Value: $_____
John Burton Collection

SAN FRANCISCO (Embossed on skirt)
Skirt: MAJESTIC BOTTLING CO. S. F.
Color: Aqua
Rarity: Common
Value: $_____
John Burton Collection

SAN FRANCISCO
Face: NEW CENTURY
        SODA WORKS
        SAN FRANCISCO
Color: Aqua
Rarity:
Value: $_____
Steve Bava Collection

SAN FRANCISCO
Face: NEW CENTURY
           SODA WORKS
           SAN FRANCISCO
Color: Green
Rarity:
Value: $_____
Steve Bava Collection

SAN FRANCISCO
Face: NEW CENTURY
           STEAM
           SODA WORKS
           SAN FRANCISCO
Color: Aqua
Rarity:
Value: $_____
Steve Bava Collection

SAN FRANCISCO
Face: OCEANO WATER
                    REG.
          AQUAMARINE CO.
          SAN FRANCISCO
Color: Aqua
Rarity:
Value: $_____
Steve Bava Collection

SAN FRANCISCO (4-ounce variant)
Face: OCEANO WATER
                    REG.
          AQUAMARINE CO.
          SAN FRANCISCO
Skirt: NET CONTENTS 4 OUNCES
Color: Aqua
Rarity:
Value: $_____
Steve Bava Collection

SAN FRANCISCO
Face: OCEANO WATER
                   REG.
            AQUAMARINE CO.
            SAN FRANCISCO
Skirt: NET CONTENTS 12 OUNCES
Color: Aqua
Rarity:
Value: $_____
Steve Bava Collection

SAN FRANCISCO
Face: P. SOMPS
          SODA WATER
            WORKS
           S. F. CAL.
Color: Aqua
Flat Base
Rarity:
Value: $_____

John Burton Collection
Left Side Bottle 8 ounce
Right Side Bottle 10 ounce

SAN FRANCISCO
Face: P. SOMPS
          SODA WATER
            WORKS
          SODA WATER
            S. F. CAL.

Color: Aqua
Rounded Base
Rarity:
Value: $_____

Steve Bava Collection
Bottle has "waves" separating script

SAN FRANCISCO
Face: PARNASBUS SODA WORKS
              (In Horseshoe)
                 (Star)
              SAN FRANCISCO

Color: Aqua
Rarity:
Value: $_____
Steve Bava Collection

SAN FRANCISCO
Face: PEERLESS

          GINGER ALE CO.

             S. F.

Color: Aqua

Rarity:

Value: $_____

Steve Bava Collection

SAN FRANCISCO Circle
Face: PIONEER

       SODA WATER CO.

          S. F.

Color: Aqua

Rarity:

Value: $_____

Steve Bava Collection

184

SAN FRANCISCO
Face: PIONEER

          SODA WATER CO.
                S. F.
Color: Aqua
Rarity:
Value: $_____
Steve & Christy Curtiss Collection

SAN FRANCISCO
Face: PIONEER
          SODA WORKS.
          W in Shield
Color: Aqua
Rarity:
Value: $_____
Steve Bava Collection

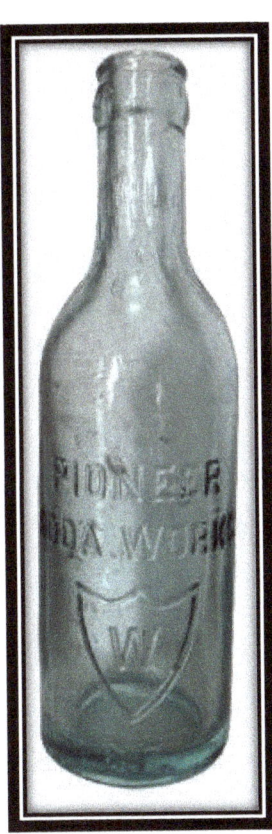

SAN FRANCISCO
Face: POPULAR
          SODA WATER
             Co.
             S.F.
Color: Aqua
Rarity:
Value: $_____
Steve & Christie Curtiss Collection

SAN FRANCISCO
Face: PURE WATER CO.
          P B Co.
          SAN FRANCISCO
Color: Aqua
Rarity:
Value: $_____
Steve Bava Collection

SAN FRANCISCO
Face: WESTERN BOTTLING COMPANY

                SF.   CAL.
Color: Aqua
Rarity:
Value: $_____
Steve Bava Collection

SAN FRANCISCO
Face: WESTERN BOTTLING COMPANY

                SF.   CAL.
Color: Aqua
Rarity:
Value: $_____
Steve & Christie Curtiss Collection

SAN FRANCISCO
Face: SAN FRANCISCO
        SODA WORKS
Color: Aqua
Rarity:
Value: $_____
Top Bottle
Bob Voegtly Collection

SAN FRANCISCO
Skirt: SAN FRANCISCO
        SODA WORKS
Color: Aqua
Rarity:
Valur $_____
Steve Bava Collection

SAN FRANCISCO

Face: SAN FRANCISCO
          SODA WORKS

Color: Aqua
Rarity:
Value: $_____
Steve & Christie Curtiss Collection

SAN FRANCISCO

Face: SCOTT & GILBERT
Base: SAN FRANCISCO
               U.S.A.

45 Ecker St. between Stevenson & Jessie
Color: Amber
Rarity:
Value: $_____
Bob Voegtly Collection

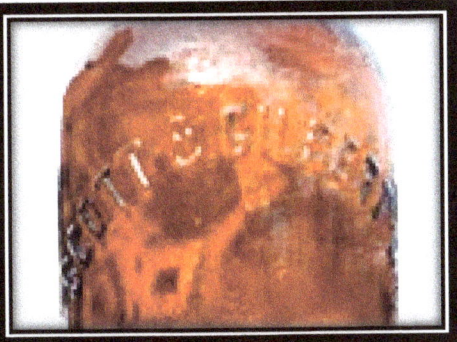

SCOTT & GILBERT CO.
mfg chemists, drugs, carbonated
beverages, flavoring extracts, shoe
dressings, writing inks, etc. 45 Ecker
bet Stevenson and Jessie, tel Douglas 1264

SAN FRANCISCO
Face: STANDARD
          HIGH GRADE
          GOODS
          SODA
          WATER CO.
          S. F. CAL.
Color: Aqua
Rarity:
Value: $_____
Image

SAN FRANCISCO
Face: REFRESHMENT
             INC.
          TREASURE ISLAND
Skirt: NET CONTENTS 6 FL. OZS.
Color: Clear
Rarity: Extremely Rare
Value: $_____
Helmut & DeAnna Jordt Collection
Bottled in San Francisco by Coca Cola
who trademarked Refreshment Inc.

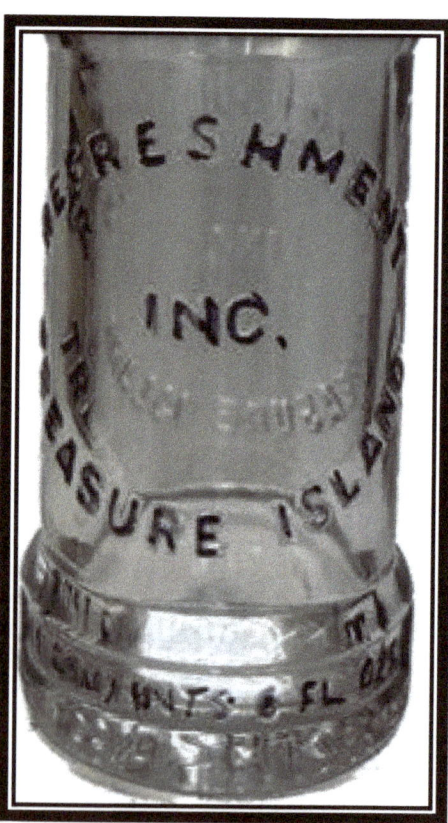

SAN FRANCISCO
Face: TWIN PEAKS
               <Twin Peaks>
           MINERAL WATER CO.
            SAN FRANCISCO

Color: Aqua
Rarity: Extremely Rare
Value: $_____
Steve Bava Collection

SAN JOSE
Face: EAGLE SODA WORKS
           R. SCHERF & SONS
            SAN JOSE, CAL.

Color: Aqua
Rarity: Rare
Value: $_____
Steve & Christie Curtiss Collection

SAN JOSE
Face: GARDEN CITY
             EXTRACT CO.
             C X Logo
             SAN JOSE
             REGISTERED
Color: Aqua
Rarity: Scarce
Value: $_____
John Burton Collection

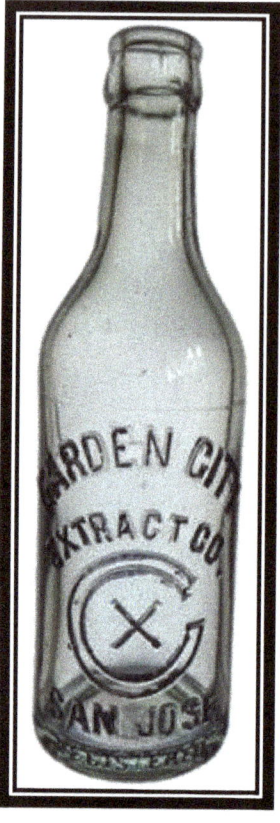

SAN JOSE
Face: MODEL EXTRACT CO.
             INC.
             MECO
             SAN JOSE, CAL.
Color: Aqua
Rarity: Scarce
Value: $_____
Steve Bava Collection

SAN JOSE
Face: GOLDEN WEST
        S & E
        SODA WORKS
        SAN JOSE
        CAL.
Color: Clear
Rarity: Scarce
Value: $_____
John Burton Collection

SAN JOSE
Face: GOLDEN WEST
        S & E
        SODA WORKS
        SAN JOSE
        CAL.
Color: Apple Green
Rarity: Scarce
Value: $_____
Steve Bava Collection

SAN JOSE
Face: GOLDEN WEST
              S & E
          SODA WORKS
            SAN JOSE
              CAL.
Color: Light Purple
Rarity: Scarce
Value: $_____
Steve & Christie Curtiss Collection

SAN JOSE
Face: SAN JOSE SODA WORKS
                 A. J.
                HENRY
            SAN JOSE, CAL.
Color: Aqua
Rarity:
Value: $_____
Steve & Christie Curtiss Collection

SAN JOSE
Face: SAN JOSE SODA WORKS
                    A. J.
                HENRY
            SAN JOSE, CAL.
Color: Sun Colored Amethyst
Rarity:
Value: $_____
Steve Bava Collection

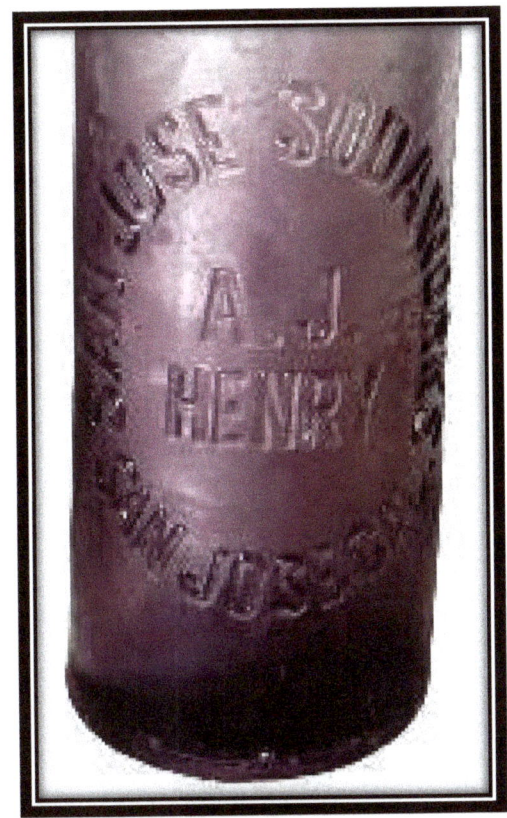

SAN JOSE
Face: SAN JOSE SODA WORKS
            JOHN BALZHAUSER
                    PROP.
            SAN JOSE, CAL.
Color: Aqua
Rarity:
Value: $_____
Steve Bava Collection

SAN JOSE
Face: QUALITY INN BRAND
REG. PAT. OFF
CHAS. J. VATH & CO.
SAN JOSE, CALIF.

Color: Aqua
Rarity: Extremely Rare
Value: $ _____
Marlon Christmann Collection

SAN JOSE
Face: WILLIAMS BROS.
W (in square)
SAN JOSE

Color: Aqua
Rarity:
Value: $_____
Steve & Christie Curtiss Collection

SAN LEANDRO

Face: SAN LEANDRO
           SODA WORKS
           SAN LEANDRO
              CAL.

Color: Aqua

Rarity:

Value: $_____

Steve & Christie Curtiss Collection

SAN LUIS

Face: BOTTLING
           San Luis
           WORKS

Color: Light Aqua

Rarity:

Value: $_____

Steve & Christie Curtiss Collection

SAN LUIS OBISPO
Face: SAN LUIS OBISPO
         SODA
         WORKS
         L. ALBERT PROP.
Color: Aqua
Rarity: Scarce
Value: $_____
Steve & Christie Curtiss Collection

SAN LUIS OBISPO (In Circle)
Face: SAN LUIS OBISPO
         SODA
         WORKS
         L. ALBERT PROP.
Color: Aqua
Rarity:
Value: $_____
Steve Bava Collection
      Tall Bottle

SAN LUIS OBISPO
Face: CROWN SODA
        WATER
        WORKS
        S. L. O.
Color: Light Purple
Rarity:
Value: $ _____
IMAGE

SAN LUIS OBISPO
Face: OTTO TULLMAN'S
        BOTTLING WORKS
        SAN LUIS OBISPO
Color: Aqua
Rarity:
Value: $_____
Stev & Christie Curtiss Collection

SAN LUIS OBISPO

Face: OTTO TULLMAN'S
             BOTTLING WORKS
             SAN LUIS OBISPO
             NET CONTENTS 8 OZS.

Color: Aqua
Rarity:
Value: $_____
Stev & Christie Curtiss Collection

SAN MATEO

Face: HIGHLAND
             GINGER ALE CO.
             SAN MATEO, CAL.

Color: Aqua
Rarity: Semi Common
Value: $_____
Steve & Christie Curtiss Collection

SAN MATEO
Face: HIGHLLAND
            GINGER ALE CO.
            SAN MATEO, CAL.
Color: Apple Green
Rarity: Rare
Value: $_____
Steve Bava Collection

SAN PEDRO (Half Circle
Face: SAN PEDRO WHOLESALE CO.
                SAN PEDRO, CAL.
Color: Aqua
Rarity:
Value: $_____
Steve Bava Collection

SAN RAFAEL
Face: MARIN
           BOTTLING WORKS
           E. MALZ
           PROP.
           SAN RAFAEL
           CAL.

Color: Clear
Rarity: Semi Rare
Value: $_____
John Burton Collection

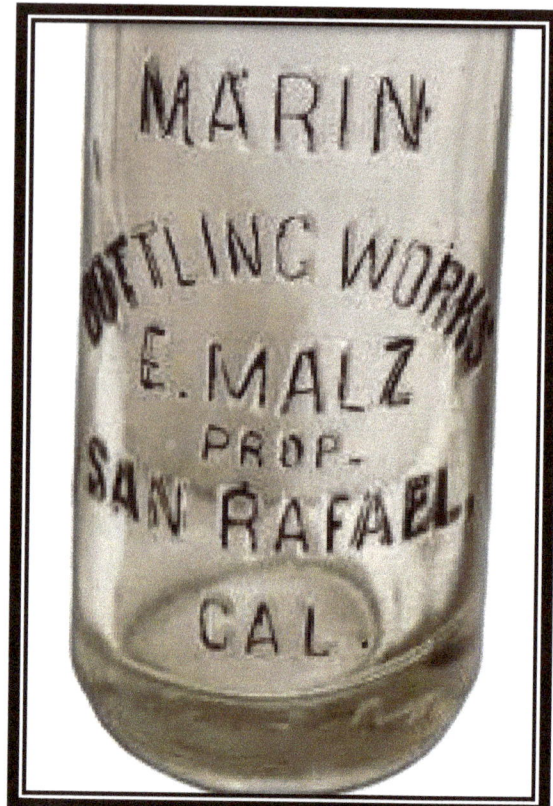

SAN RAFAEL
Face: BORRELO BROS
           TRADE B. B MARK
           SAN RAFAEL
           CAL.

Bottom: B. B.
Color: Aqua
Rarity: Scarce
Value: $_____
John Burton Collection

SAN RAFAEL

Face: BORRELO BROS

          TRADE B. B MARK

          SAN RAFAEL

            CAL.

Bottom: B. B.

Color: Aqua

Rarity: Scarce

Value: $_____

John Burton Collection

SANTA ANA

Face: G. W. WELLS

            W

         SANTA ANA

Color: Aqua

Rarity:

Value $_____

Steve & Christie Curtiss Collection

SANTA ANA
Face: W

Color: Aqua
Rarity:
Value $_____
Steve Bava Collection

SANTA ANA
Face: GRUMBACH
&
SCHUMACHER
SANTA ANA
CAL.
Color: Aqua
Rarity:
Value $_____
Steve & Christie Curtiss Collection

SANTA ANA
Face: GRUMBACH
&
SCHUMACHER
SANTA ANA
CAL.
Color: Sun Colored Amethyst
Rarity:
Value $_____
Steve Bava Collection

SANTA ANA
Face: SCHUMACHER & SCHUMACHER
SANTA ANA
Color: Aqua
Rarity:
Value: $_____
Steve & Christie Curtiss Collection

SANTA BARBARA
Face: LAGOMARCHINO-PARMA CO.
          SANTA BARBARA

Color: Aqua
Rarity:
Value: $_____
Steve Bava Collection

SANTA BARBARA
Face: MISSION SODA WORKS
          JOS. TAPIE
          PROP.
          SANTA BARBARA

Color: Clear
Rarity: Very Rare
Value: $_____
Marlon Christmann Collection

SANTA BARBARA
Face: MISSION SODA WORKS
        SANTA BARBARA, CAL.
Color: Aqua
Rarity: Scarce
Value: $_____
Steve & Christie Curtiss Collection

SANTA BARBARA (In Circle)
Face: SANTA BARBARA
        SODA WORKS
        SANTA BARBARA
Color: Light Amber
Rarity:
        8 Ounce
Value: $_____
Steve & Christie Curtiss Collection

SANTA BARBARA (In Circle)
Face: SANTA BARBARA
          SODA WORKS
          SANTA BARBARA
Color: Light Aqua
Rarity:
      12 Ounce
Value: $_____
Steve & Christie Curtiss Collection

SANTA CLARA
Face: OLYMPIA SODA WATER WORKS
          JAS. PEREIRA
          & CO.
          SANTA CLARA, CAL.
Color: Sun Colored Amethyst
Rarity:
Value: $_____
Steve Bava Collection

SANTA CLARA

Face: SANTA CLARA SODA WORKS
            DAVIS & CO.
            SANTA CLARA

Color: Aqua
Rarity:
Value: $_____
Steve & Christie Curtiss Collection

SANTA CRUZ

Face: EAGLE

       SODA WATER
         AND
      BOTTLING CO.
    SANTA CRUZ, CAL.

Color: Aqua
Rarity: Very Rare
Value: $_____
Steve Bava Collection

SANTA CRUZ

Face: SANTA CRUZ
J. J.
SODA WORKS
SANTA CRUZ
CAL.

Color: Aqua
Rarity:
Value: $_____
Steve & Christie Curtiss Collection

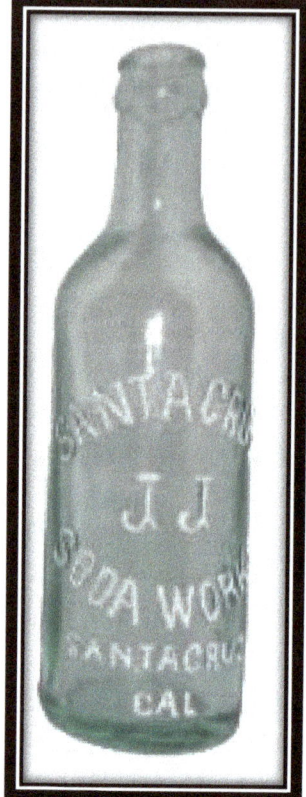 

SANTA MARIA

Skirt: SANTA MARIA
SODA WORKS

Color: Aqua
Rarity:
Value: $_____
Steve Bava Collection

 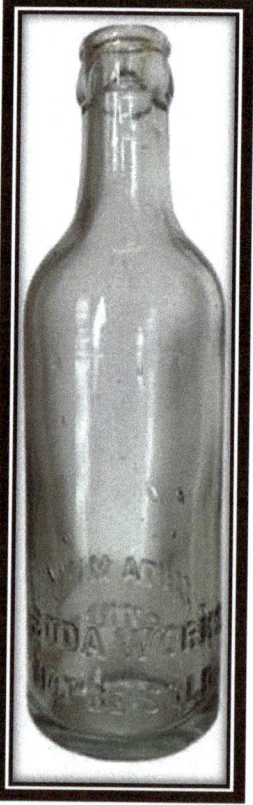  

SANTA MARIA

Skirt: SANTA MARIA SODA WORKS
           THIS BOTTLE MUST BE RETURNED
Color: Light Purple
Rarity:
Value: $_____
Steve & Christie Curtiss Collection

SANTA MONICA

Skirt: SANTA MONICA
Reverse: IMPERIAL ICE CO.
Color: Aqua
Rarity:
Value: $_____
Marlon Christmann Collection

SANTA ROSA
Face: ROSE CITY SODA WORKS
          MATHEWS
                  &
          ROBERTS
          SANTA ROSA. CAL.
Color: Aqua
Rarity: Common
Value: $_____
John Burton Collection

SANTA ROSA
Face: ROSE CITY SODA WORKS
          JAS. L. ROBERTS
          SANTA ROSA. CAL.
Color: Aqua
Rarity: Common
Value: $_____
John Burton Collection

SANTA ROSA

Face: REGISTERED
SANTA ROSA BOTTLING CO.
SRBCO
SANTA ROSA, CAL.

Color: Aqua
Rarity: Extremely Rare
Value: $_____
Transition bottle from hutch to crown
John Burton Collection

SANTA ROSA

Face: SANTA ROSA BOTTLING CO.
SRBCO
SANTA ROSA, CAL.
REGISTERED

Color: Aqua
Rarity: Common
Value: $_____
John Burton Collection

SANTA ROSA
Face: SANTA ROSA BOTTLING CO.
SRBCO
SANTA ROSA, CAL.
REGISTERED
Color: Light Sun Colored Amethyst
Rarity: Semi Common
Value: $_____
John Burton Collection

SANTA ROSA
Face: SANTA ROSA BOTTLING CO.
SRBCO
SANTA ROSA, CAL.
REGISTERED
Color: Deep Sun Colored Amethyst
Rarity: Semi Common
Value: $_____
Steve Bava Collection

SANTA ROSA
Face: SANTA ROSA
          SODA WORKS
Color: Clear
Rarity:
Value: $_____
John Burton Collection

SANTA ROSA
Face: O.C.
            BEVERAGES
            7 FL. OZ.
Reverse: PAT'D
            JULY 20, 1920
            ORANGE
            CRUSH CO.
            BOTTLE
Bottom: SANTA ROSA, CAL.
Color: Clear
Rarity: Common
Value: $_____
John Burton Collection

SANTA ROSA

Face: ROSE
                BOTTLING WORKS
                SANTA ROSA, CAL.

Reverse: CITY
                E. BROWN
                NET CONTENTS 9 OZ.

Bottom: E. BROWN & SON

Color: Clear

Rarity: Semi Rare

Value: $_____

John Burton Collection

SANTA ROSA

Face: WHISTLE
                REGISTERED
                PAT. NO. 70843, 1926

Reverse: WHISTLE
                6 ½ FLD. OZS.
                REG. U.S.

Bottom: SANTA ROSA, CAL.

Color: Clear

Rarity: Semi Common

Value: $_____

John Burton Collection

SANTA ROSA
Face: NEHI
                BEVERAGES
                SANTA ROSA, CAL.
Reverse: NEHI
                REG. U. S. PAT.OFF
                NEHI BOTTLING CO.
Bottom: DESIGN PAT.D MAR. 3
Color: Clear
Rarity: Extremely Common
Value: $_____
John Burton Collection

SANTA ROSA
Face: BIG ONE
        SANTA ROSA BOTTLING WORKS
              REGISTERED
Reverse: SANTA ROSA
          NET CONTENTS 7 OZ.
Color: Clear
Rarity: Common
Value: $_____
John Burton Collection

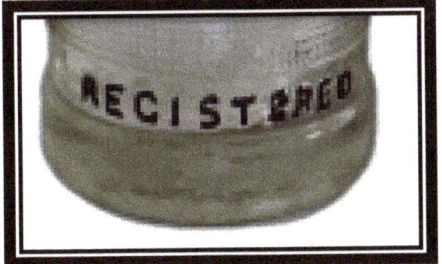

SANTA ROSA
Face: NU GRAPE
          A FLAVOR YOU CAN'T FORGET
          NOT GRAPE JUICE
          MIN. CONTENTS 6 FLD. OZ.
Reverse: NU GRAPE
          A FLAVOR YOU CAN'T FORGET
          IMITATION GRAPE
          TRADE MARK REGISTERED
          BOTTLE PAT'D MARCH 9, 1920
Bottom: SANTA ROSA, CAL.
Color: Apple Green
Rarity: Extremely Rare
Value: $_____
John Burton Collection

SANTA ROSA
Face: GRACE BROS. SANTA ROSA, CAL.
          GRACE BROS.
          ARTIFICAL COLOR ADDED
          AND FLAVOR FRUIT ACID ADDED
          CONTENTS 9 FLUID OZS. REGISTERED
Reverse: GRACE BROS.
                GB
Color: Clear
Rarity: Semi Common
Value: $_____
John Burton Collection

SANTA ROSA (Embossed & Painted Label)
Face: GRACE BROS.
          ARTIFICAL FLAVOR
          FRUIT ACID ADDED
Reverse: GRACE BROS.
          NET CONTENTS
          9 FLD. OZS.
Bottom: 4213G
          GB
          20<o>6

Color: Clear
Rarity: Semi Common
Value: $_____
John Burton Collection

SANTA ROSA & SEBASTOPOL
Face: MIN. CONTENTS 6 FLD. OZS.
          DELAWARE
          PUNCH
Left Side: NON-ALCOHOLIC
          IMITATION PUNCH
          ARTIFICAL COLOR
          AND FLAVOR
Right Side: DELAWARE

          TRADE MARK
          REGISTERED
          BENZGATE OF SODA
          TRACE
Bottom: SANTA ROSA

          SEBASTOPOL
Color: Green
Rarity: Very Rare
Value: $_____
John Burton Collection

SANTA ROSA

Face: MIN. CONTENTS 6 FLD. OZS.
        DELAWARE
        PUNCH
Left Side: NON-ALCOHOLIC
        IMITATION PUNCH
        ARTIFICAL COLOR
        AND FLAVOR
Right Side: DELAWARE
        PUNCH

        TRADE MARK
        REGISTERED
Bottom:

        S. R.
Color: Clear
Rarity: Semi Rare
Value: $_____
John Burton Collection

SANTA ROSA & SEBASTOPOL

Face: COCA COLA
Reverse: TRADE MARK REGISTERED
        NET CONTENTS 6 FLD. OZS.
        COCA COLA
        TRADE MARK REGISTERED
        BOTTLE PAT'D NOV. 16, 1915
Bottom: SANTA ROSA
              &
        SEBASTOPOL
Color: Coca Cola Green
Rarity: Extremely Rare
Value: $_____
John Burton Collection

SANTA ROSA
Face: Hires Paper Label
BOTTOM: W. H. HUDSON
Color: Clear
Rarity: Very Rare
Value: $_____
John Burton Collection

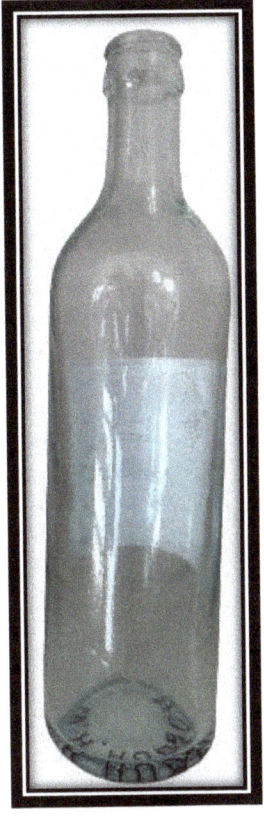

SARATOGA
Face: PACIFIC
             CONGRESS
             SPLITS
Color: Aqua
Rarity:
Value: $_____
Steve Bava Collection

SARATOGA (Embossed on Base)
Bottom   PACIFIC
               CONGRESS
               WATER
Color: Green
Rarity:
Value: $_____
Steve Bava Collection

SARATOGA
Face: PACIFIC
             CONGRESS SPRINGS
                  MINERAL
                   WATER
          SARATOGA, CALICORNIA
Color: Aqua
Rarity:
Value: $_____
Steve & Christie Curtiss Collection

SEBASTOPOL (Vertical Embossing)
Face: SEBASTOPOL
         BOTTLING WORKS
          SEBASTOPOL
Color: Aqua
Rarity: Very Rare
Value: $_____
John Burton Collecrion

SEBASTOPOL
Face: ENTERPRISE
         SODA WORKS
         SEBASTOPOL
         Color: Aqua
Rarity: Very Rare
Value: $_____
Merle Avila Collection

SEBASTOPOL Half Circle
Face:　ENTERPRISE
　　　　SEBASTOPOL
　　　　BOTTLING WORKS
Color:　Aqua
Rarity:　Scarce
Value:　$_____
John Burton Collection

SEBASTOPOL (Embossed on bottom)
Bottom:　ENTERPRISE BOTTLING
　　　　SEBASTOPOL
　　　　WORKS
Color:　Aqua
Rarity:　Very Rare
Value:　$_____
John Burton Collection

SEBASTOPOL
Face: CRYSTAL
             BOTTLING CO.
             SEBASTOPOL
             CAL.
Color: Clear
Rarity:
Value: $_____
John Burton Collection

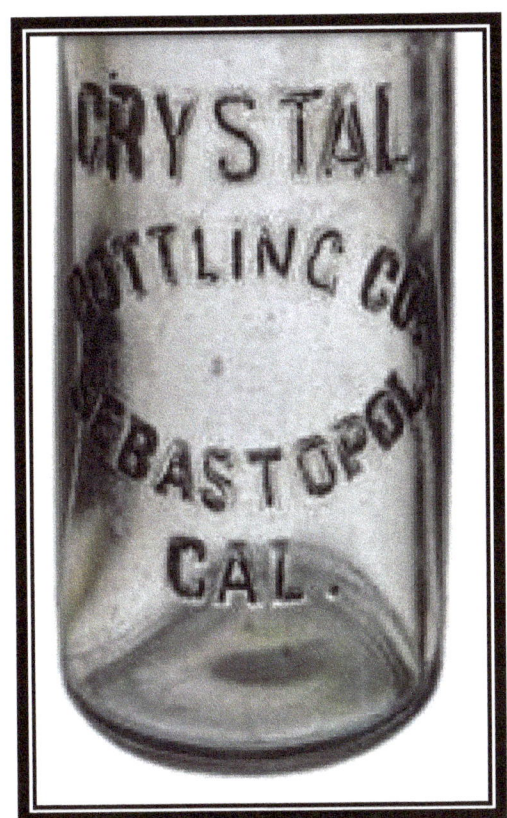

SEBASTOPOL
Face: CRYSTAL
             BOTTLING CO.
             SEBASTOPOL
             CAL.
Color: Aqua
Rarity:
Value: $_____
Merle Avila Collection

SEBASTOPOL
Face: COCA COLA
Reverse: TRADE MARK REGISTERED
          NET CONTENTS 6 FLD. OZS.
          COCA COLA
          TRADE MARK REGISTERED
          BOTTLE PAT'D NOV. 16, 1915
Bottom: SEBASTOPOOL (Misspelt)
          CAL.
Color: Coca Cola Green
Rarity: Extremely Rare
Value: $_____
Merle Avila Collection

SELMA
Face: MORGAN & CO.
           SELMA
           CAL.
Color: Aqua
Rarity:
Value: $_____
Steve & Christie Curtiss Collection

SELMA
Face: PERFECTION SODA WORKS
                SELMA, CAL.
Color: Sun Colored Amethyst
Rarity:
Value: $_____
Steve Bava Collection

SHASTA (Vertical Embossing)
Face: SHASTA
          GINGER ALE
Color: Aqua
Rarity:
Value: $_____
Steve Bava Collection

SHASTA (Vertical Embossing)
Face: SHASTA
Color: Aqua
Rarity:
Value: $_____
Steve & Christie Curtiss Collection

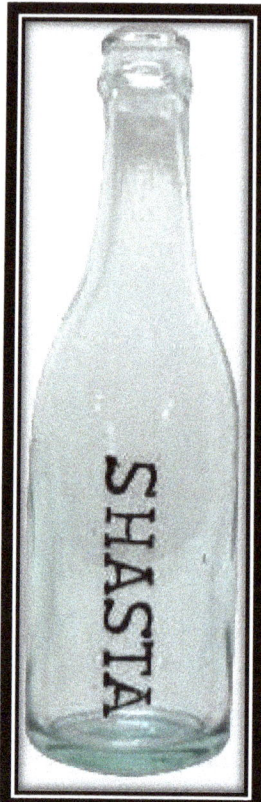 

SHASTA (Vertical Embossing)
Face: SHASTA
        WATER
Color: Amber
Rarity:
Value: $_____
John Burton Collection

SHASTA (Skirt Embossed)
Skirt: "SHASTA" WATER CO.
Color: Aqua
Rarity: Common
Value: $_____
Steve Bava Collection

SHASTA (Skirt Embossed)
Skirt: SHASTA
         WATER CO.
Color: Aqua & Sun Colored Amethyst
Rarity:
Value: $_____
Steve & Christie Curtiss Collection

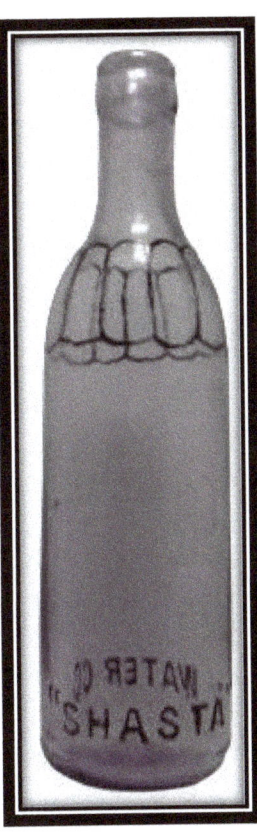

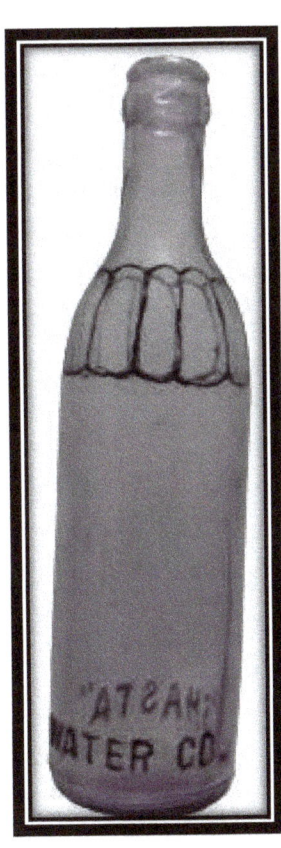

SHASTA COUNTY

Face: THE LOWER
                SODA SPRINGS
                SHASTA CO.
                     CAL.

Color: Aqua
Rarity:
Value: $_____
Steve Bava Collection

SISSON

Face: MUGLER BROS.
                SISSON, CAL.
        THIS BOTTLE NEVER SOLD

Color: Aqua
Rarity:
Value: $_____
Steve & Christie Curtiss Collection

SISSON
Face: PETER MUGLER
             BREWER
             SISSON
             CAL.

Color: Aqua
Rarity:
Value: $_____
Steve Bava Collection

SONOMA
Face: STAR SODA WORKS
             ★
             SONOMA CAL.
Bottom: ★
Color: Aqua
Rarity: Semi Common
Value: $_____
John Burton Collection

SONOMA

Face: SONOMA VALLEY SODA
        WORKS
        ARTIFICAL COLOR AND
        FLAVOR
        FRUIT ADDED
        CONTENTS 8 FLUID OZS.

Color: Clear
Rarity: Scarce
Value: $_____
John Burton Collection

SONORA

Face: BACON'S
        SODA WORKS
        SONORA,
        CAL.

Color: Aqua
Rarity: Scarce
Value: $_____
Horizonal Embossing
Steve & Christie Curtiss Collection

SONORA
Face: BACON'S
          SODA WORKS
            SONORA
               CAL.
Color: Aqua
Rarity: Very Scarce
Value: $_____
Steve & Christie Curtiss Collection

SONORA
Face: SAMMONS
          SODA WORKS
            SONORA
               CAL.
Color: Aqua
Rarity:
Value: $_____
Steve Bava Collection

SONORA

Face: M. TERZICH
         SONORA
         CAL.

Color: Aqua

Rarity: Scarce

Value: $_____

Steve Bava Collection

SONORA

Skirt: Embossed on Base
         M. TERZICH
         SONORA, CAL.

Color: Aqua

Rarity: Scarce

Value: $_____

SONORA
Face: TERZICH'S
            GOOD SODA
            ORANGE
            FLAVORED
            SONORA, CAL.
Color: Clear
Rarity:
Value: $_____

SONORA
Face: THOMAS LEONARD
            SONORA
            SODA WORKS
            SONORA, CAL.
Color: Aqua
Rarity:
Value: $_____
Image

SONORA
Face: LEONARD
          SONORA
             CAL.
Color: Aqua
Rarity:
Value: $_____
Steve Bava Collection

SONORA
Face: LEONARD's
          SONORA
             CAL.
Color: Aqua
Rarity:
Value: $_____
Steve & Christie Curtiss Collection

ST. HELENA
Face: ST. HELENA
        SODA
        &
        B. B. Co.
Color: Amethyst
Rarity:
Value: $_____
John Burton Collection

ST. HELENA
Face: ST. HELENA
        SODA WORKS
        ST. HELENA, CAL.
Color: Aqua
Rarity:
Value: $_____
Steve Bava Collection

ST. HELENA
Face: ST. HELENA BOTTLING
           AND
           COLD STORAGE CO.
           ST. HELENA
           CAL.

Color: Aqua
Rarity:
Value: $_____
Dan Brown Collection

ST. HELENA
Face: ST. HELENA BOTTLING
           AND
           COLD STORAGE CO.
           ST. HELENA
           CAL.
           CONTENTS 7 FLD. OZ.

Color: Aqua
Rarity:
Value: $_____
John Burton Collection

STOCKTON
Face: C. BARTELS
        (Hands Clasped)
        STOCKTON
Color: Aqua
Rarity:
Value: $_____
Steve & Christie Curtiss Collection

STOCKTON
Face: C. BARTELS
        Clasped Hands
        STOCKTON
Color: Aqua
Rarity:
Value $_____
Steve Bava Collection

STOCKTON
Face: REGISTERED
          MODEL SODA WORKS
          Hands clasped
          STOCKTON
          CAL.
Color: Aqua
Rarity: Very Scarce
Value: $_____
Steve & Christie Curtiss Collection

STOCKTON
Face: J. S. WAGNER
        STOCKTON, CALIF.
Color: Aqua
Rarity:
Value: $_____
Steve & Christie Curtiss Collection

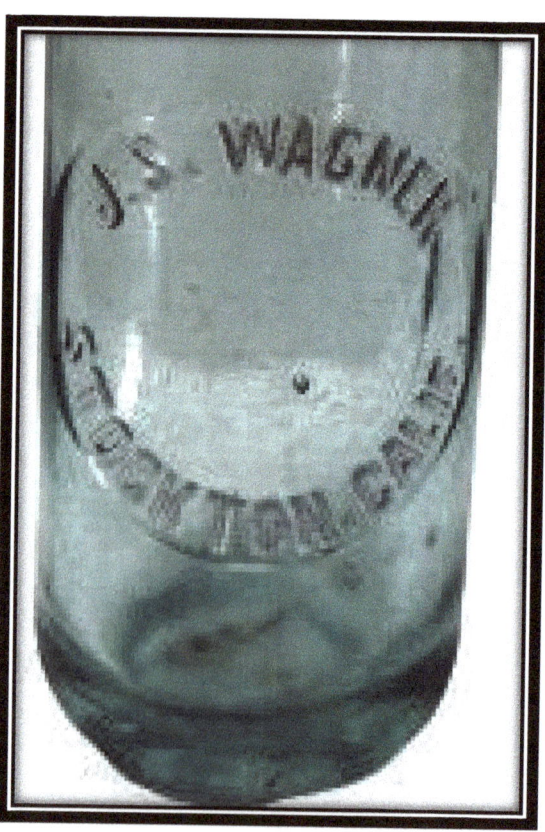

STOCKTON
Face: N (National)
Color: Aqua
Rarity:
Value: $_____
Bob Voegtly Collection

STOCKTON
Face: N (National)
Color: Sun Colored Amythyst
Rarity:
Value: $_____
Steve Bava Collection

STOCKTON

Face: NATIONAL SODA WORKS
           Horseshoe
           STOCKTON
              CAL.

Color: Purple
Rarity:
Value: $_____
Steve & Christie Curtiss Collection

STOCKTON

Face: NATIONAL SODA WORKS
            Horseshoe
            STOCKTON
              CAL.

Color: Aqua
Rarity:
Value: $_____
Steve & Christie Curtiss Collection

STOCKTON
Face: PEARSON'S
           SODA WORKS
Color: Aqua
Rarity:
Value: $_____
Steve Bava Collection

STOCKTON
Face: STOCKTON
          SODA WATER CO.
            P. & P.
          STOCKTON, CAL
Color: Aqua
Rarity:
Value: $_____
Steve & Christie Curtiss Collection

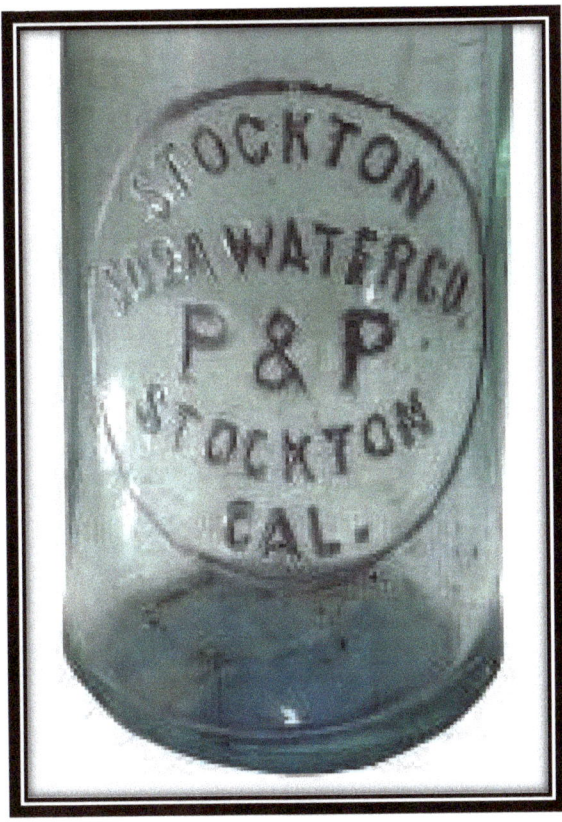

STOCKTON
Face: STOCKTON SODA
          WORKS
        H. E. MOLEN
      STOCKTON, CAL
Color: Aqua
Rarity:
Value: $_____
Steve & Christie Curtiss Collection

SUISUN
Face: NECTAR
       BOTTLING
       WORKS
      SUISUN, CAL.
Color: Clear
Rarity:
Value: $_____
Steve Bava Collection

SUISUN

Face: SUISUN ICE AND SODA WORKS
SUISUN, CAL.

Color: Aqua
Rarity:
Value: $_____
Steve & Christie Curtiss Collection

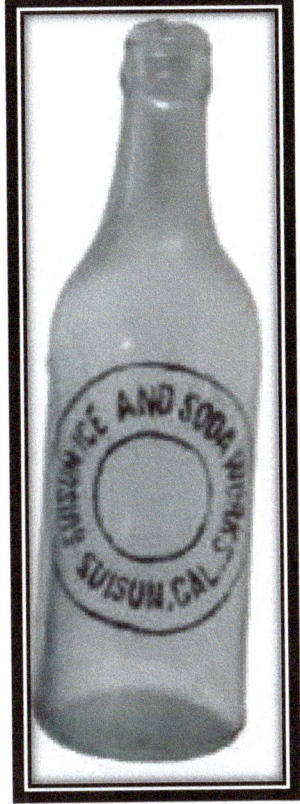 

SUMNER & BAKERSFIELD

Face: G. GALLI
SODA WORKS
SUMNER
&
BAKERSFIELD

Color: Aqua
Rarity: Very Scarce
Value $_____
Image

TAFT
Face: WEST SIDE
              BOTTLING WORKS
              TAFT, CALIF.
              BOTTLE NEVER SOLD

Color: Aqua
Rarity:
Value: $_____
Steve & Christie Curtiss Collection

TRACY
Face: TRACY SODA WORKS
              TRACY, CAL.

Color: Aqua
Rarity:
Value: $_____
Steve & Christie Curtiss Collection

TULARE
Face: TULARE SODA
       WORKS
       TULARE, CAL.
Color: Aqua
Rarity:
Value: $_____
Marlon Christmann Collection

TUOLUMNE (Oval)
Face: TUOLUMNE SODA WORKS
       TUOLUMNE, CAL.
Color: Aqua
Rarity: Scarce
Value: $_____
Steve & Christie Curtiss Collection

TURLOCK
Face: TURLOCK SODA
           WORKS
           TURLOCK, CAL.
Color: Aqua
Rarity:
Value: $_____
Image

UKIAH
Face: UKIAH ICE & BREWING CO.
           <Barrel>
           UKIAH, CAL.
Color: Aqua
Rarity:
Value: $_____
Does barrel relate to Root Beer?
John Burton Collection

UKIAH

Face: UKIAH ICE & BREWING CO.
<Barrel>
UKIAH, CAL.

Color: Sun Colored Amethyst

Rarity:

Value: $_____

Does barrel relate to Root Beer?

John Burton Collection

VACAVILLE

Face: SOLANO
VACAVILLE

Color: Aqua

Rarity:

Value: $_____

Steve Bava Collection

VACAVILLE
Face: SOLANO SODA WORKS
          VACAVILLE,
                 CAL.
Color: Aqua
Rarity:
Value: $_____
Steve Bava Collection

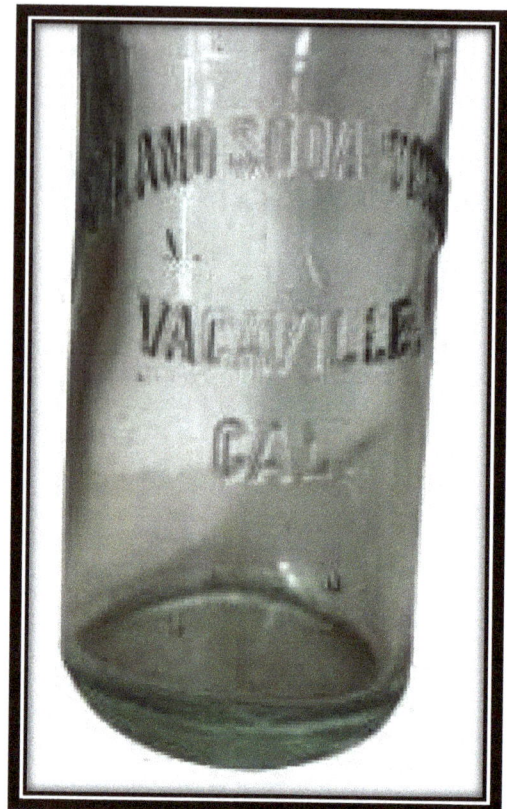

VACAVILLE
Face: SOLANO SODA
          & ICE WORKS
          VACAVILLE
          NET CONTENTS
          9 FL. OUNCES
Color: Aqua
Rarity:
Value: $_____
John Burton Collection

VACAVILLE
Face: SOLANO SODA
      & ICE WORKS
      VACAVILLE
      NET CONTENTS
      7 FL. OUNCES

Color: Aqua
Rarity:
Value: $_____
Steve & Christie Curtiss Collection

VACAVILLE
Face: TOLENAS
      SODA
      SPRINGS
Reverse: TOLENAS
      SODA
      SPRINGS

Color: Aqua
Rarity:
Value: $_____
Marlon Christmann Collection

VALLEJO
Face: EMPIRE
           SODA WORKS
           VALLEJO, CAL.
Color: Aqua
Rarity: Semi Common
Value: $_____
John Burton Collection

VALLEJO
Face: EMPIRE SODA WORKS
           VALLEJO
Color: Aqua
Rarity: Semi Common
Value: $_____
Steve Bava Collection

VALLEJO

Face: ST. LOUIS BOTTLING CO.
           McC. & B.
           VALLEJO CAL.

Color: Aqua
Rarity:
Value: $_____
Steve Bava Collection

VENTURA

Face: ACME SODA WORKS
           M & S. CO.
           VENTURA, CAL.

Color: Aqua
Rarity: Very Scarce
Value $_____
Steve & Christie Curtiss Collection

VENTURA

Color: Aqua
Rarity: Very Scarce
Value $_____
Steve & Christie Curtiss Collection

VISALIA
Face: M. MOONEY
            VISALIA
Color: Aqua
Rarity: Rare
Value: $_____
Image

VISALIA
Face: VISALIA
             CONTENTS
             8 FLUID OUNCES
             SODA WORKS
Color: Aqua
Rarity:
Value: $_____
Steve & Christie Curtiss Collection

 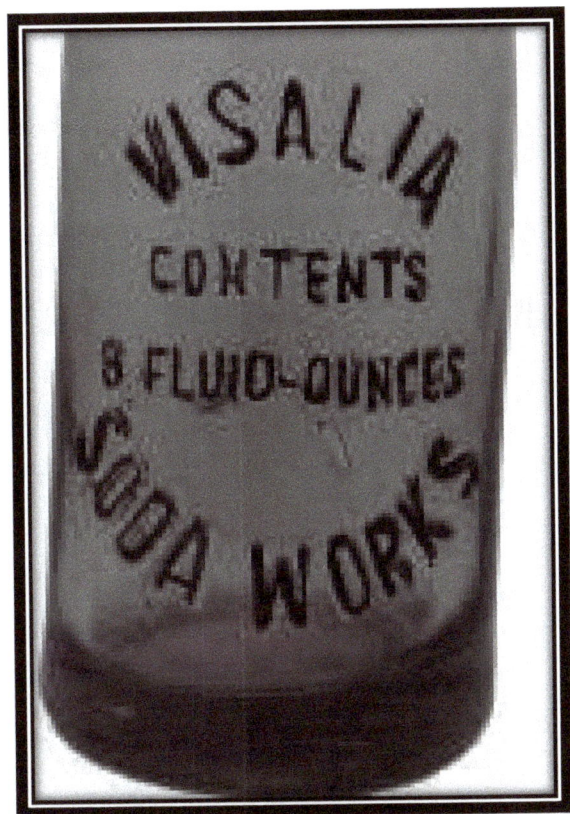

VISALIA
Face: VISALIA
             SODA WORKS
Color: Aqua
Rarity:
Value: $_____
Steve & Christie Curtiss Collection

VISALIA
Face: VISALIA
           SODA WORKS
Color: Green
Rarity:
Value: $_____
Steve Bava Collection

WALNUT GROVE
Face: LION SODA WORKS
          (Lion)
          WALNUT GROVE
Color: Clear
Rarity:
Value: $_____
Steve & Christie Curtiss Collection

WATSONVILLE
Face: S. MARTINELLI
                   S. M.
           WATSONVILLE, CAL.

Color: Aqua
Rarity:
Value: $_____
Steve Bava Collection

WATSONVILLE (Vertical)
Face: THE
       PRETTYMAN-WOLF CO.
         WATSONVILLE
            CAL.

Color: Aqua
Rarity:
Value: $_____
Steve & Christie Curtiss Collection

WATSONVILLE

Face: WATSONVILLE
         BOTTLING WORKS
         H. A. P.
         PROPRIETOR
Color: Aqua
Rarity:
Value: $_____
Steve Bava Collection

WATTS

Face: I. FIELDS & SON
         WATTS, CAL.
Color: Aqua
Rarity:
Value: $_____
Steve Bava Collection

WESTWOOD

Face: THE RED RIVER LUMBER CO.
          MERCANTILE DEPT.
        PAUL BUNYAN'S Head
             PINE

Skirt: NET CONTENTS 6½ FLUID OUNCES

Color: Clear

Rarity:

Value: $_____

Helmut & DeAnna Jordt Collection

WILLITS

Face: WILLITS
        SODA WORKS
         WILLITS, CAL.

Color: Aqua

Rarity:

Value: $_____

John Burton Collection

WILLOWS

Face:
WILLOWS
SODA WORKS
WILLOWS In horse shoe
CAL.

Color: Aqua
arity:
Value: $_____
Steve & Christie Curtiss Collection

WINTHROP

Face:
F. W. ZEIS
WINTHROP

Color: Aqua
Rarity: Scarce
Value: $_____
Steve & Christie Curtiss Collection

WINTHROP

Face: ZIES BROS.
               WINTHROP
                  CAL.

Color: Aqua
Rarity:
Value: $_____
Steve & Christie Curtiss Collection

(ZEIS misspelt)

WOODLAND

Face: J. F.
            WOODLAND
            NET CONTENTS
             7½ OZ.

Color: Aqua
Rarity: Common
Value: $_____
Marlon Christmann Collection

WOODLAND (Half circle)
Face: WOODLAND SODA
            WORKS
Color: Aqua
Rarity:
Value: $_____
Steve & Christie Curtiss Collection

YREKA
Face: MEAMBER BROS.
                BOTTLERS OF
                HIGH CLASS
                CARBONATED BEVERAGES
                ABOVE TRADE MARK
                PROTECTED
Color:
Rarity: Very Rare
Value: $_____
Mike Rouse Collection

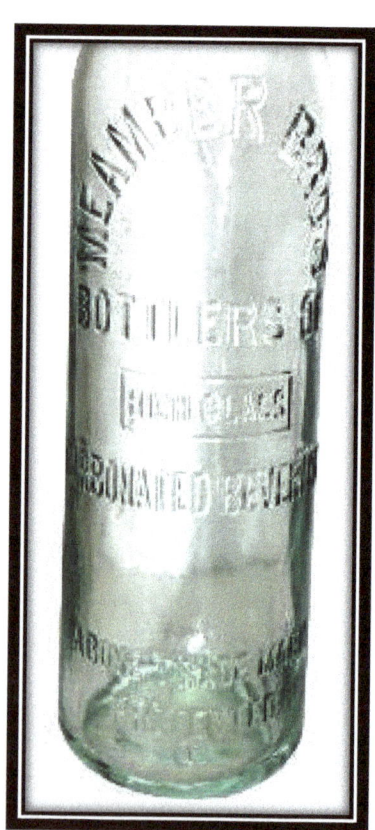

YREKA
Face: MEAMBER BROS.
                    BOTTLERS OF
                    HIGH CLASS
                    CARBONATED BEVERAGES

Color: Clear
Rarity: Very Rare
Value   &_____
Dale Mlasko Collection

YREKA
Face: MEAMBER
          YREKA CAL.
Color: Clear
Rarity: Semi Rare
Value: $_____

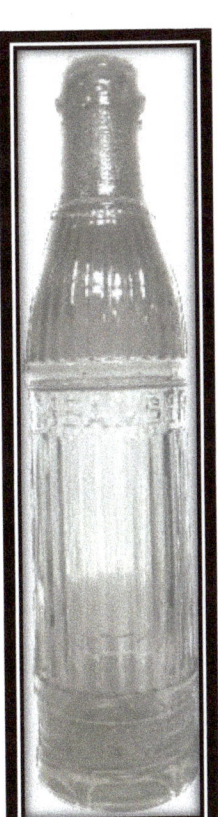

YREKA
Face: MEAMBER BROS.
          BOTTLERS
Color:
Rarity: Extremely Rare
Value: $_____
Mike Rouse Collection

YREKA
Face: JOS. STEINAGHER
          AND SON
          YREKA, CAL.
Color: Aqua
Rarity: Very Rare
Value: $_____
Steve & Christie Curtiss Collection

YREKA
Face: PARKINSON AND WISE
                YREKA

Color:
Rarity:
Value: $_____
Mike Rouse Collection

YREKA
Face: YREKA
           BOTTLING WORKS

Color:
Rarity:
Value: $_____
Mike Rouse Collection

CALIFORNIA EMBOSSED CROWN TOP BOTTLES

HAYWARDS/ SODA WORKS/ S. J. S. SIMMONS (Clear)
HAYWARDS/ SODA WORKS/ S. J. S. SIMMONS (Aqua)

F. O. BRANDT/ HEALDSBURG/ CAL.
F.B. /HEALDSBURG/ CAL.
HEMET SODA WORKS/HEMET/ CAL.
HEMET/SODA WORKS/ HEMET. CALIF.
HOLLISTER/ SODA WORKS/ HOLLISTER, CAL
VALLEY SPRINGS & SODA/ WORKS/ HOLLYWOOD/ CAIFORNIA
IONE ICE & SODA WORKS/ LAP/IONE, CAL.
J. T. SCHERRER/ JACKSON
JACKSON BOTTLING/ P&G/ WORKS
JACKSON BOTTLING/ P/ WORKS
JACKSON BOTTLING/ P/ WORKS (Fancy P)
JACKSON BOTTLING/ P/ WORKS (Sun Color Amethyst)
JACKSON/ P&T/ BOTTLING WORKS (Aqua)
JACKSON/ P&T/ BOTTLING WORKS (Clear)
JOHN STROHM/ JACKSON, CAL.
KENNETT/ BOTTLING WORKS/ J. D. COOK & SON/ PROPS.
STAR/ Star image/ KERN, CAL.
KERN/ COUNTY/ BOTTLING/ WORKS
BARTLETT/ GINGER ALE/ L. E. McMAHAN & SONS/ TRADE MARK
HIGHLAND/ MINERAL/ WATER
HIGNLAND (Vertical face)/ NATURAL/ MINERAL/ WATER
ALLEN SPRINGS CO./LAKE CO./ CALIFORNIA
LIVERMORE SODA WORKS/ (Lamb image/ LIVERMORE/ CAL.
LIVERMORE SODA WORKS/LIVERMORE/ CAL.
LIVERMORE SODA WORKS/ LSW/ LIVERMORE/ CAL.
SUPERIOR/ BOTTLING WORKS/ LONG BEACH CAL.
PEOPLES/ICE/&/COLD STORAGE/CO./LONG BEACH
ACME BOTTLING/WORKS/LOS ANGELES
ALOHA BOTTLING WORKS/ W. & S./ LOS ANGELES/ CAL.
CRYSTAL/ BOTTLING/ CBCo. /COMPANY/ LOS ANGELES

CASCADE SODA WORKS/ PEVERLY/ BROS./ PROPS. /LOS ANGELES
EXCELSIOR/ SODA WORKS/ LOS /ANGELES CAL.
F. A. HEIM'S/ BOTTLING WORKS
ELYSIAN SPRING/ WATER CO./ LOS ANGELES
HONEY CHAMPAGNE/ V. H. Co./ LOS ANGELES/ CALIF. (Image)
HYGEIA/ MINERAL WATER/ CO./ LOS ANGELES/ CAL.
LOS ANGELES/ Image of star/ SODA WORKS/ THIS BOTTLE IS REGISTERED/ NOT TO BE SOLD
LOS ANGELES/ Image of star/ SODA WORKS/ THIS BOTTLE IS REGISTERED/ NOT TO BE SOLD
LOS ANGELES ICE & COLD STORAGE/ LOS ANGELES
NEW YORK/ BOTTLING WORKS/ LOS ANGELES/ CAL.
NEW YORK/ BOTTLING WORKS/ LOS ANGELES
IDEAL BOTTLING WORKS/ LOS ANGELES, CAL.
PROPERTY OF THE/ PURITAS/ L. A.L. & C. S. CO./ LOS ANGELES/ BOTTLE NOT TO BE SOLD
THE ICE & COLD/ STORAGE Co./ PURITAS/ OF/ LOS ANGELES/ THIS BOTTLE/ IS NOT SOLD
LOS ANGELES/ ICE & COLD STORAGE CO./ BOTTLE IS NOT SOLD
RAMONA/ BOTTLING/ WORKS/ LOS ANGELES, CAL.
RAMONA/ LOS ANGELES/ BOTTLING WORKS
SHAW OF CALIFORNIA/ Monogram/HIGH GRADE/ BEVERAGES/ LOS ANGELES & VENTURA
WHITE STAR/ SODA WORKS/ LOS ANGELES, CAL.

LOS BANOS/ I & B/ SODA WORKS (Circle)
LOS BANOS/ I & B/ SODA WORKS (Half Circle)
LOS BANOS/ JACOPI & BROS./ SODA WORKS
LOS BANOS/ SODA WORKS
LOS BANOS SODA WORKS/ LOS BANOS (On bottom of bottle)
LOS GATOS SODA WKS./ L. M./ LOS GATOS
LOS GATOS SODA WKS./ (Image of cat) LOS GATOS, CAL./NET CONTENTS 8 OZS.
BORELLO & PORTER/ MADERA
J. G. PORTER/ BOTTLING WORKS/ MADERA, CAL.
Alhambra/ GINGER ALE/ ALHAMBRA/ NATURAL/ MINERAL WATER CO./ MARTINEZ/ CAL.
ALHAMBRA/ MINERAL WATER/ BOTTLED AT THE SPRINGS
A.N.M.W. CO./TRADE MARK/REGISTERED/NET CONTENTS 7 OZ./ Alhambra/ MARTINEZ, CAL
A.N.M.W. CO./ TRADE MARK/ REGISTERED/ Alhambra/ MARTINEZ, CAL.
XLCR/ SODA (Star in shield) WORKS/ MARTINEZ
B (Belden) Aqua
B (Belden) Apple Green
B & M (Embossed on Bottom)
CAL. BOTTLING WKS./ MARYSVILLE
MARYSVILLE/ M. S. W./ CAL. (Embossed on Bottom)
YUBA/ BOTTLING WORKS/ MARYSVILLE, CAL.

G. M. W. / R. B.

JOS. HOEFER/ SODA WORKS/ REDDING

ZEIS & SONS CO./ REDDING CAL./ THIS BOTTLE IS NEVER SOLD

ZEIS & SONS/ REDDING CAL.

REDLANDS BOTTLING/ WORKS/ J. T. ALLEN PROP.

REDWOOD CITY SODA WATER CO./ REWOOD CITY

HEANEY BROS./ REDWOOD CITY CAL.

HIGHLAND/ GINGER ALE/REDWOOD CITY, CAL.

YOSEMITE/ SODA WORKS/ REDWOOD CITY

RICHMOND SODA WORKS/ R.S.W./ RICHMOND

RICHMOND SODA WORKS/ R S W / POINT RICHMOND

RICHMOND SODA WORKS/ R S W in blocked script / POINT RICHMOND

RIVERSIDE SODA WORKS/ RIVERSIDE CAL. Embossed bottom skirt (Aqua)

RIVERSIDE SODA WORKS/ RIVERSIDE CAL. Embossed bottom skirt (Apple Green)

O. K. BOTTLING Co./ RIVERSIDE

ROSEVILLE/ SODA WATER BOTTLING/ WORKS/ CONTENTS 8 OZS.

ROSEVILLE/ SODA WATER BOTTLING/ WORKS/ CONTENTS 8 OZS.

ARISTO/ MINERAL WATER/ AND/ SIPHON CO./ SACRAMENTO/ CAL.

ARISTO/ARISTO (Near bottle neck)

ARISTO/ SACRAMENTO (On bottle base)

C. SCHNERR & CO./ SACRAMENTO/ CAL./ TRADE MARK REGISTERED/ BOTTLE IS NEVER SOLD
CAPITOL SODA WORKS (on bottom)

C. SCHNERR & CO./ SACRAMENTO/ CAL./ TRADE MARK REGISTERED/ BOTTLE IS NEVER SOLD

C. SCHNERR & CO./ SACRAMENTO/ CAL./ TRADE MARK REGISTERED/ BOTTLE IS NEVER SOLD

SCHNERR/ SAC-CAL

SILVER GATE/ SCHNEER/ BROS./ SODA WORKS

CALIFORNIA/ BOTTLING WORKS/ T. BLAUTH/ 407 K STREET/ SACRAMENTO

CALIFORNIA/ BOTTLING WORKS/ T. BLAUTH & SONS/ 407 K STREET/ SACRAMENTO

GROSJEAN & HOLDAWAY/ Monogram/ SACRAMENTO/ CAL.

GROSJEAN & HOLDAWAY/ Monogram/ SACRAMENTO/ CAL.
Reverse – *COCA COLA*/ TRADE MARK/ REGISTERED

S.C.O.N.M.W. ASSN./ SACRAMENTO

LEWIS DELEW/ BOTTLER/ SACRAMENTO, CAL.

THIS BOTTLE/ IS THE PROPERTY OF/ LEWIS DELEW/ BOTTLER/ SACRAMENTO, CAL. (Aqua)

THIS BOTTLE/ IS THE PROPERTY OF/ LEWIS DELEW/ BOTTLER/ SACRAMENTO, CAL. (Purple)

SUN RISE SODA WORKS/ (Sun Rise)/ SACRAMENTO CAL (Muddy Green)

SUN RISE SODA WORKS/ (Sun Rise) SACRAMENTO CAL. (Aqua)

THE GEO. Z. WAIT/ CARBONATING/ CO/ SACRAMENTO. CAL. (Sun Colored Amethyst)
WHITE STAR SODA WKS./ (Star) SACRAMENTO
WILSON HALL & Co./ SACRAMENTO/ CAL.
WILSON MF'G CO./ HIGH GRADE/ CARBONATED DRINKS/ SACRAMENTO/ CAL./
ABOVE TRADE MARK/ PROTECTED
BOTTLE NOT SOLD/ WILSON MFG. CO./ W. M. CO./ SACRAMENTO
WILSON MFG. CO./ SACRAMENTO, CAL./ BOTTLE NOT TO BE SOLD

SALINAS
SALINAS/ SODA WORKS/ SALINAS CAL.
SALINAS SODA WORKS/ P. STEIGELMAN/ SALINAS, CAL./ BOTTLE NEVER SOLD (Aqua)
SALINAS SODA WORKS/ P. STEIGELMAN/ SALINAS, CAL./ BOTTLE NEVER SOLD (Apple Green)
PARAISO MINERAL WATER/ BOTTLED BY/ P. STEIGELMAN/ SALINAS. CAL
SALINAS BOTTLING WORKS/ B & M/ SALINAS/ CAL. (Apple Green)
SALINAS BOTTLING WORKS/ B & M/ SALINAS/ CAL. (Aqua)

SAUSALITO
MASON & CO./ SAUSALITO, CAL.
MASON/ SODA WORKS/ SAUSALITO (Aqua – Vertical)
MASON/ SODA WORKS/ SAUSALITO (Light Purple – Vertical)
MASON/ SAUSALITO/ GINGERALE (Aqua – Vertical)
WHISTLE/ 6½ FLD. OZS. / REG. U.S./ (SAUSALITO, CAL. on Bottom)
DRINK/ MASON'S/ SODA/ ITS COOL
Meyer's
Meyer's/ SPECIAL/ CONTENTS 10 FL. OZS.
B & H

SAN ANSELMO
SAN ANSELMO/ BOTTLING CO./ SAN RAFAEL, CAL.
SAN ANSELMO/ BOTTLING/ Co./ SAN RAFAEL/ CAL.

SAN BERNARDINO
EXCELSIOR BOTTLING/ WORKS/ SAN BERNARDINO
SAN BERNARDINO/ S & S/ EAGLE SODA WORKS
SAN BERNARDINO SODA WORKS (Embossed on skirt)

SAN DIEGO
EXCELSIOR/ BOTTLING WORKS/ SAN DIEGO/ CAL.
MONARCH SODA WORKS/ Lions Head image/ A. HAYDIS & SON/ SAN DIEGO/ CAL.
SAN DIEGO/ TRADE (Star) MARK/ SODA WORKS (Apple Green)
SAN DIEGO/ TRADE (Star) MARK/ SODA WORKS (Aqua)
THE/ DISTILLED WATER/ AND/ BOTTLING CO./ SAN DIEGO, CAL.
SILVER GATE/ SCHEPP/ BROS./ SODA WORKS
BRADLEY/SPRING WATER/ Eagle/SAN DIEGO, CAL.
Rex/ Bottling Co./ San Diego

SAN FRANCISCO
ALTA BOTTLING CO./ 22nd AVE & T ST./ SAN FRANCISCO
AMERICAN/Flag Image/MINERAL WWATER CO./S.F.
AMERICAN/ Flag image/SODA WORKS/ S.F

BAY CITY SODA WATER CO./ SAN FRANCISCO/ CAL./ REGISTERED (Light Green)
BAY CITY SODA WATER CO./ SAN FRANCISCO/ CAL./ REGISTERED (Aqua)
BELFAST/ TRADE B MARK/ GINGER ALE/ S.F.
B/ BELFAST/ 7 FL. OZ.
CALIFORNIA/ PURE WATER CO./ (Logo)/ SAN FRANCISCO (Light Green)
CALIFORNIA/ PURE WATER CO./ (Logo)/ SAN FRANCISCO (Aqua)
CALIFORNIA/ PURE WATER CO./ (Logo)/ SAN FRANCISCO (Amber)
CLUB/SODA/ (Reverse) MADE FROM/ NATURAL MINERAL/ WATER/ Re-Carbonated
CROWN/ Crown image/ J.J. BLIVEN & CO/ SODA WATER/ COMPANY/ SAN FEANCISCO, CAL.
Crown image/ SODA WORKS
Crown image/ SODA WORKS
CROWN/ SODA WATER CO./ S. F.
CROWN/ SODA WATER CO./S. F. / JAS. BLIVEN & CO.
DIAMOND SODA WORKS/ SAN FRANCISCO
EGGERS & CO./ FINE BEVERAGES/ S. F. CAL.
ENTERPRISE/ SODA WORKS/ S. F.
ENTERPRISE SODA WORKS/ SAN FRANCISCO
EUREKA- CALIFORNIA/ Eagle image/ SODA WATER CO./ S.F. (Aqua)
EUREKA- CALIFORNIA/ Eagle image/ SODA WATER CO./ S.F. (E-C on bottom)
EUREKA- CALIFORNIA/ Eagle image/ SODA WATER CO./ S.F. (Amber)
GOLDEN WEST/ SODA WORKS/ SAN FRANCISCO/ CAL. (Aqua) Horseshoe on bottom
GOLDEN WEST/ SODA WORKS/ SAN FRANCISCO/ CAL. (Greenish Yellow) Horseshoe on bottom
MAJESTIC BOTTLING CO. S. F. (Embossed on skirt)
NEW CENTURY/ SODA WORKS/ SAN FRANCISCO (Aqua)
NEW CENTURY/ SODA WORKS/ SAN FRANCISCO (Apple Green)
NEW CENTURY/ STEAM/ SODA WORKS/ SAN FRANCISCO
OCEANO WATER/ REG./ AQUAMARINE CO./ SAN FRANCISCO (4 Ounce variant)
OCEANO WATER/ REG./ AQUAMARINE CO./ SAN FRANCISCO
P. SOMPS/ MINERAL WATER/ NAPA COUNTY/ CAL.
P. SOMPS/ SODA WATER/ WORKS/ S.F. CAL.
P. SOMPS/ SODA WATER/ WORKS/ S. F. CAL, (Fancy script)
P. SOMPS/ SODA WATER/ WORKS/ S. F. CAL. (Vertical)
PARNASSUS SODA WORKS inside horseshoe/ (Star) /SAN FRANCISCO
PEERLESS/ GINGER ALE CO./ S.F.
PIONEER/ (Bear image)/ SODA WATER CO./ S.F.
PIONEER/ SODA WATER/ W in shield
POPULAR/ SODA WATER/ CO./ S.F.
PURE WATER CO./ PBCo Monogram/ SAN FRANCISCO
WESTERN BOTTLING COMPANY inside horseshoe/ S. F. CAL. (Aqua)
WESTERN BOTTLING COMPANY inside horseshoe/ S. F. CAL. (Apple Green)
SAN FRANCISCO/ SODA WORKS
SAN FRANCISCO/ SODA WORKS on bottom of bottle
SAN FRANCISCO/ SODA WORKS (Tall bottle)
SCOTT & GILBERT/ SAN FRANCISCO/ U.S.A.(Amber)

STANDARD/ HIGH GRADE/ GOODS/ SODA/ WATER CO, / S. F. CAL.
REFRESHMENT/INC./TREASURE ISLAND/NET CONTENTS 6 FL. OZS.
TWIN PEAKS/ (Twin Peaks image) MINERAL WATER CO./ SAN FRANCISCO.

SAN JOSE
EAGLE SODA WORKS/ SCHERF & SON/ SAN JOSE, CAL.
GARDEN CITY/ EXTRACT CO./CX/ SAN JOSE/ REGISTERED
MODEL EXTRACT CO./ INC./ MECO logo/ SAN JOSE, CAL
GOLDEN WEST/ S & E/ SODA WORKS/ SAN JOSE/ CAL. (Clear)
GOLDEN WEST/ S & E/ SODA WORKS/ SAN JOSE/ CAL. (Apple Green)
GOLDEN WEST/ S & E/ SODA WORKS/ SAN JOSE/ CAL. (Light Purple)
SAN JOSE SODA WORKS/ A. J./ HENRY/ SAN JOSE, CAL. (Aqua)
SAN JOSE SODA WORKS/ A. J./ HENRY/ SAN JOSE, CAL. (Sun Colored Amethyst)
SAN JOSE SODA WORKS/ JOHN BALZHAUSER/ PROP. / SAN JOSE, CAL.
QUALITY INN BRAND/ REG-PAT-OFF/ CHAS. J. VATH & CO./ SAN JOSE, CALIF,
WILLIAMS BROS./ W in box/ SAN JOSE

SAN LEANDRO
SAN LEANDRO/ SODA WORKS/ SAN LEANDRO/ CAL.

SAN LUIS OBISPO
BOTTLING/ San Luis/ WORKS
SAN LUIS OBISPO/ SODA/ WORKS/ L. ALBERT PROP.
SAN LUIS OBISPO/ SODA/ WORKS/ L. ALBERT PROP. (Tall Bottle)
CROWN SODA/ WATER/ WORKS/ S. L. O.
OTTO TULLMAN'S/ BOTTLING WORKS/ SAN LUIS OBISPO
OTTO TULLMAN'S/ BOTTLING WORKS/ SAN LUIS OBISPO/ NET CONTENTS 8 OZS.

SAN MATEO
HIGHLAND/ GINGER ALE CO./ SAN MATEO, CA. (Aqua)
HIGHLAND/ GINGER ALE CO./ SAN MATEO, CA. (Apple Green)

SAN PEDRO
SAN PEDRO WHOLESALE CO./ SAN PEDRO, CAL.

SAN RAFAEL
MARIN/ BOTTLING WORKS/ E. MALZ/ PROP. / SAN RAFAEL, CAL.
BORELLO BROS./ TRADE B.B MARK/ SAN RAFAEL/ CAL. (B.B. on bottom)
BORELLO BROS./ TRADE B.B MARK/ SAN RAFAEL/ CAL. (Sloped shoulders)

SANTA ANA
G.W. WELLS/ W/ SANTA ANA
W
GRUMBACH/ &/ SCHUMACHER/ SANTA ANA/ CAL. (Aqua)
GRUMBACH/ &/ SCHUMACHER/ SANTA ANA/ CAL. (Sun Colored Amethyst)
SCHUMACHER & SCHUMACHER/ SANTA ANA

SANTA BARBARA
LAGOMARCHINO – PARMA CO./ SANTA BARBARA
MISSION SODA WORKS/ JOS. TAPIE/ PROP. / SANTA BARBARA
MISSION SODA WORKS/ SANTA BARBARA, CAL. (Aqua)

MISSION SODA WORKS/ SANTA BARBARA, CAL. (Light Amber)
MISSION SODA WORKS/ SANTA BARBARA, CAL. (Light Aqua)

OLYMPIA SODA WATER WORKS/ JAS. PEREIRA/ & CO./ SANTA CLARA. CAL.
SANTA CLARA SODA WORKS/ DAVIS & CO./ SANTA CLARA
EAGLE/Eagle image/ SODA WATER/ AND/ BOTTLING CO./ SANTA CRUZ, CAL.
SANTA CRUZ/ J.J./ SODA WORKS/ SANTA CRUZ/ CAL.
SANTA MARIA/ SODA WORKS (Embossed on skirt) (Aqua)
SANTA MARIA/ SODA WORKS (Embossed on skirt) (Light Purple)
SANTA MONIA/ IMPERIAL ICE (Embossed on skirt)
ROSE CITY SODA WORKS/ MATHEWS/&/ ROBERTS/ SANTA ROSA. CAL
ROSE CITY SODA WORKS/ JAS. ROBERTS/ SANTA ROSA. CAL.
REGISTERED/ SANTA ROSA BOTTLING CO./ Monogram SRBCO/ SANTA ROSA. CAL.
SANTA ROSA BOTTLING CO./ SRBCO./ SANTA ROSA. CAL./ REGISTERED (Aqua)
SANTA ROSA BOTTLING CO./ SRBCO./ SANTA ROSA. CAL./ REGISTERED (Sun Colored Amethyst
SANTA ROSA BOTTLING CO./ SRBCO./ SANTA ROSA. CAL./ REGISTERED (Purple)
SANTA ROSA/ SODA WORKS
O. C. BEVERAGES/ 7 FL. OZ.
ROSE/ BOTTLING WORKS/ SANTA ROSA, CAL. – Reverse CITY/E. BROWN/ NET CONTENTS
                    9 OZ./ E. BROWN & SON on bottom of bottle
WHISTLE/ REGISTERED/ PAT. NO. 70843, 1926 -Reverse WHISTLE 6 ½ FLD. OZS ./REG. U. S. /
                    SANTA ROSA, CAL
NEHI/ BEVERAGES/ SANTA ROSA, CAL. Reverse NEHI/ REG. U. S. PAT.OFF/ NEHI BOTTLING CO./
                    DESIGN PAT.D MAR 3
BIG ONE/ SANTA ROSA BOTTLING WORKS/ REGISTERED/ Reverse – NET CONTENTS 7 OZ.
NU-GRAPE/ A FLAVOR YOU CAN'T FORGET/ NOT GRAPE JUICE/ MIN. CONTENTS 6 FLD. OZ./
                    NU-GRAPE/ A FLAVOR YOU CAN'T FORGET/ NOT GRAPE JUICE/
                    TRADE MARK REGISTERED/BOTTLE PAT'D MARCH 9, 1920
                    SANTA ROSA on bottom of bottle
GRACE BROS. SANTA ROSA, CAL. / GRACE BROS. / ARTIFICAL COLOR ADDED/ AND FLAVOR
             FRUIT ADDED/ CONRENTS 9 FLUID OZS. REGISTERED – Reverse GRACE BROS./ GB
GRACE BROS./ ARTIFICAL FLAVOR/ FRUID ACID ADDED/ Reverse- GRACE BROS. / NET
                    CONTENTS/ 0 FLD. OZS. Bottom 4213G/ GB/ 20<0>
MIN. CONTENTS 6 FLD. OZS./ DELAWARE PUNCH/ SANTA ROSA-SEBASTOPOL
MIN. CONTENTS 6 FLD. OZS./ DELAWARE PUNCH/ S. R.
COCA COLA/ Bottom of bottle SANTA ROSA & SEBASTOPOL
On bottom of bottle W. H. HUDSON (William H. Hudson Santa Rosa Soda Works)
PACIFIC/ CONGRESS/ SPLITS
Embossed on bottom – PACIFIC/ CONGRESS/ WATER

PACIFIC/ CONGRESS SPRINGS/ MINERAL/ WATER/ SARATOGA, CALIFORNIA

SEBASTOPOL/ BOTTLING WORKS/ SEBASTOPOL (Vertical)
ENTERPRISE/ BOTTLING WORKS/ SEBASTOPOL
ENTERPRISE/ SEBASTOPOL/ BOTTLING WORKS
Embossed on bottom ENTERPRISE BOTTLING/ SEBASTOPOL. WORKS
CRYSTAL/ BOTTLING CO./ SEBASTOPOL/ CAL.
COCA COLA/ SEBASTOPOOL (Sebastopol misspelt)
MORGAN & CO./ SELMA/ CAL.
PERFECTION SODA WORKS/ SELMA. CAL.
SHASTA/ GINGER ALE (Vertical)
SHASTA/ SHASTA (Vertical)
SHASTA/ WATER (Vertical) Amber
SHASTA WATER CO. Embossed on skirt
SHASTA/ WATER CO. Embossed on skirt (Sun Colored Amethyst)
THE LOWER/ SODA SPRINGS/ SHASTA CO./CAL.
MUGLER BROS./ SISSON, CAL./ THIS BOTTLE NEVER SOLD
PETER MUGLER/ BREWER/ SISSON/ CAL.
STAR SODA WORKS/ Star/ SONOMA CAL.
SONOMA VALLEY SODA WORKS/ ARTIFICAL COLOR AND FLAVOR/ FRUIT ADDED/
                                CONTENTS 8 FLUID OZS.
BACON'S/ SODA WORKS/ SONORA/ CAL.
BACON'S/ SODA WORKS/ SONORA/ CAL. (Arch)
SAMMONS/ SODA WORKS/ SONORA/ CAL.
M. TERZICH/ SONORA/ CAL.
M. TERZICH/ SONORA CAL. Etched on bottom of bottle
TERZICH'S/ GOOD SODA/ ORANGE FLAVORED/ SONORA, CAL
THOMAS LEONARD/ SONORA/ SODA WORKS/ SONORA, CAL.
LEONARD/ SONORA/ CAL.
LEONARD'S/ SONORA/ CAL.
ST. HELENA/ SODA/ &/ B.B. CO.
ST. HELENA/ SODA WORKS/ ST. HELENA, CAL.
ST. HELENA BOTTLING/ AND/ COLD STORAGE CO./ ST. HELENA/ CAL./ CONTENTS 7 FLD. OZS.
BARTELS/ Hands Clasped/ STOCKTON
BARTELS/ Hands Clasped) STOCKTON

REGISTERED/ MODEL SODA WORKS/ Hands Clasped/STOCKTON/ CAL.
J. S. WAGNER/ STOCKTON, CALIF.
N (National) Aqua
N (National) Sun Colored Amythyst
NATIONAL SODA WORKS/ Horseshoe/ STOCKTON/ CAL. (Purple)
NATIONAL SODA WORKS/ Horseshoe/ STOCKTON/ CAL. (Aqua)
PEARSON'S / SODA WORKS
STOCKTON/ SODA WATER CO./ P. & P./ STOCKTON/ CAL.
STOCKTON SODA/ WORKS/ H. E. MOLEN/ STOCKTON, CAL.
STOCKTON / SODA WATER CO./ P. & M./ STOCKTON/ CAL.

VISALIA/ SODA WORKS

VISALIA / SODA WORKS

LION SODA WORKS/ Lion Head/ WALNUT GROVE

S. MARTINELLI/ S. M. / WATSONVILLE, CAL.

THE/ PRETTYMAN-WOLF CO./WATSONVILLE, CAL. (Vertical)

WATSONVILLE/ BOTTLING WORKS/ H. A. P./ PROPRIETOR

I. FIELDS & SON/ WATTS, CAL

THE RED RIVER LUMBER CO./ MERCANTILE DEPT./ PAUL BUNYAN'S (Head)/PINE

WILLITS/ SODA WORKS/ WILLITS, CAL.

WILLOWS/ SODA WORKS/ WILLOWS/ CAL.

F. W. ZEIS/ WINTHROP

ZIES BROS/ WINTHROP/ CAL. (Zeis misspelt)

J.F./ WOODLAND/ NET CONTENTS/ 7½ OZ.

WOODLAND SODA/ WORKS

MEAMBER BROS./ BOTTLERS OF/ HIGH CLASS/ CARBONATED BEVERAGES/
                    ABOVE TRADE MARK/ PROTECTED

MEAMBER BROS./BOTTLERS/ HIGH CLASS/ CARBONATED BEVERAGES

MEAMBER/YREKA CAL.

MEAMBER BROS./ BOTTLERS

JOS. STEINAGHER/ AND SON/ YREKA, CAL.

PARKINSON AND WISE/ YREKA

YREKA/ BOTTLING WORKS

SOMPS HISTORY

YESTERDAY'S FIRE.
A Chapter of Accidents and Narrow Escapes

Several narrow escapes from death occurred at the fire which broke out early yesterday morning at the soda works of Pierce & Somps, at 259 and 261 Clementina Street. (Who was Pierce?)

The employes' lodgings were in the front of the building, and when the fire broke out Francis Retif, father-in-law of Mr. Somps, was almost suffocated by the smoke that gathered in bis room. It was only by the help of a lad named Wm. Theme that he escaped unhurt.

Jean Laborde was also caught in the room, and when he tried to escape was so stifled by the hot air that he could only reach the door, where be lost consciousness and fell down. He was rescued by some fireman. Laborde was desperately burned about the face, neck and bands. He was taken to a neighboring house and attended to until removed to the French Hospital by his lodge, the Franco-American Lodge, I. O. O. F. He is in a very critical condition.

Chief Scannell was unusually unfortunate on Saturday night. At a fire earlier in the evening he was knocked down by a horse and slightly bruised; at the soda works some acid exploded and the Chief was plentifully bespattered with the flying drops. Though not much scalded, yet his hair has assumed a sea-green tinge wherever touched by the acid. The loss and insurance on the buildings destroyed were given in Sunday's issue of the Alta.
April 25, 1887 Daly Alta California

Damages for Malicious Prosecution.
Moritz Weinberg commenced suit yesterday against P. G. Somps, alleging that on the 18th instant Somps caused his arrest on the charge of receiving stolen property; without probable cause, and he was imprisoned in the City Prison for three hours. He asked judgment against Somps for $5,000 damages done to his credit and reputation by reason of said alleged false' arrest and imprisonment.
March 24,1889 Daly Alta California

Damages For Malicious Arrest
In the suit of Moritz Weinberg against P. G. Somps for malicious prosecution the jury yesterday rendered a verdict in favor of the plaintiff for $3,333. Somps had Weinberg arrested as a receiver of stolen property, but failed to sustain the charge before the Police Court. Weinberg then sued for $5,000 damages and a jury gave him the above verdict.
March 26, 1889 Daly Alta California

The Body Identified

On Sunday the body of a drowned man was found on Baker's Beach, south of Fort Point. Yesterday the body was identified by Peter Somps as that of his brother, John Somps, who so mysteriously disappeared three weeks ago from 259 Clementina Street.

He was a native of France, a teamster by occupation, and aged thirty-five years. He was a single man, and, it is stated, was soon to have been married to Miss Eugenia Duprey. His brother has no idea why Somps committed suicide, if it was a case of suicide.

February 20, 1890 Daly Alta California

SOMPS VS. JOHN D. TAYLOR

Suit has been begun against John D. Taylor, proprietor of the Pioneer Soda Works at Thirteenth and Webster Streets, for $20,000 damages.

P. G. Somps, proprietor of the Steam Soda Works of San Francisco, is the plaintiff. He alleges that for ten years he has been engaged in manufacturing and bottling in syphon soda bottles, a certain kind of soda water. His bottles have been etched with his trade-mark. The defendant, he alleges, has been manufacturing soda water and been using the same bottles for two years past, representing that his product is manufactured by the plaintiff.

May 4, 1891 Daly Alta California

RIVAL SODA MEN.
They Take Their Grievances into the Police Court.

There is a bitter feeling between P. G. Somps and M. Mouret & Co., rival soda water manufacturers, which has been carried into the Police Court. Yesterday morning Mr. Somps swore out warrants in Judge Low's court for the arrest of three of Mouret & Co.'s drivers, John Lacon, Dennis Bellgarde and John Barrare, on a felony charge of stealing his siphon bottles.

Mr. Somps said that the drivers of Mouret & Co.'s wagons had been gathering up his bottles, breaking them and selling the lead. Last year 3,000 bottles, worth $1 each, had disappeared in that way. A few days ago, some of Somps' men dressed themselves in shabby clothing and went to Mouret & Co.'s establishment on Montgomery Street, near Jackson, representing themselves as rag and bottle men. They found a barrel filled with broken bottles belonging to Somps.

On Tuesday Somps obtained a search warrant. He accompanied the officer to Mouret & Co.'s, amt they discovered a large number of his bottles packed under some hay. Yesterday he swore out the warrants for the arrest of the three drivers. He threatens to bring Mouret before the Grand Jury.   February 7, 1895 San Francisco Call

P. G. Somps Accuses His Rivals of Breaking Bottles.

P. G. **Somps** has brought a rather peculiar suit for damages against Marcelin Mouret, Jean Bassere and Jean Lecour. The persons named are rivals in the soda water business, and the plaintiff alleges that the defendants have been collecting the bottles which he has been delivering to his customers and destroying them. Each bottle, he says, is worth .85 cents, and already the defendants have destroyed 3,000 of them. They are still at work upon his bottles, he says, and so asked that they be restrained from further breakage as well as compelled to pay him $5,000 damages for that already done.   March 1, 1895 Call

P. G **Somps** has sued Denis Bellegarde, and the latter has been told to stop collecting siphon bottles marked "Steam Soda Works" or "S. S. W."

April 21, 1895 Call

RECEIVING STOLEN GOODS

Mouret, Soda Water Manufacturer, 'Held on Two Charges.

The long drawn out; case of M. Mouret, soda water manufacturer, 815 Montgomery Street, charged on the complaint of P. G. Somps, soda water manufacturer, with; receiving stolen goods, was concluded before' Judge Cbalari yesterday, aftcrnoon. Mouret, it was shown by the evidence, had been. buying Somps' bottles which had been stolen by different people, and: had either broken them up or else utilized them himself or disposed of the faucets. A private detective was employed by Somps to watch Mouret' place, and his arrest was the result. The Judge after carefully reviewing the evidence held; Mouret to answer before the Superior Court on 2 (two) charges in $1000 bonds on each charge.

February 11, 1896 San Francisco Call

SOMPS AND HIS REVOLVER.
The Soda Water Merchant Causes a Panic in a Saloon.

Emile Somps, a soda water merchant, who has a somewhat dangerous proclivity for brandishing a' loaded revolver occasionally, has been placed under police surveillance for an exhibition of his dexterity with the weapon in the Auditorium saloon Thursday; evening. He entered the saloon early in the evening, and after a few words with Louis Fichter, one of the proprietors, on business affairs — Fichter having at one time been a customer of Somps in the purchase of soda water — began to abase the saloonkeeper for not continuing to deal with him.

Fichter paid no attention to him and Somps seeing that talking was of no avail deliberately spat upon him. This exasperated Fichter, and he reached behind the counter for a bottle to use as a weapon. Somps seeing, and mistaking the meaning of the move, drew a revolver and threatened to shoot. Although the word most uttered nowadays and most thought of is war, firearms in the nature of revolvers have little attraction or fascination for frequenters of saloons, and in a moment, there were about a dozen or more revelers, including the barkeeper himself making a mad rush for the door. Upon gaining the street Somps quickly and mysteriously disappeared.

May 14, 1898 San Francisco Call

"COLONEL" BRADY LANDS ON SOMPS' SOLAR PLEXUS

"COLONEL" BRADY, the well-known fighter has at last won a fight. He has a record of fifty battles, forty-nine of which he lost. The other was declared a draw on account of police interference. The first man to fall a victim to his terrible right or "a booze destroyer" as lie is won't to term it, is Emile Somps, who is a familiar figure on the "line."

Friday night Brady and Somps had a dispute which culminated in the Colonel challenging his adversary to put on the gloves with him. Somps, who is over six feet tall and who has acquired considerable muscle through handling bottles at his father's soda works, thinking the Colonel was a "puddin'," as he expressed it. readily accepted the deal.

In order to make the bout more interesting Somps offered to bet $20 that he would put Brady to sleep in two rounds. The Colonel promptly covered the bet, and accompanied by several friends, they repaired to the Olympic Club, where they completed arrangements for the "scrap." After considerable wrangling "Billy" Kennedy was selected as referee. Eight-ounce gloves were used; as Brady did not want to take a chance of having his face disfigured.

At the tap of the bell Somps, who knows something about the game through his associations with the Alameda Terror, and other prize fighters of equal prominence, started to annihilate Brady. The Colonel cleverly dodged several wicked swings by falling to the floor and staying down the allotted ten seconds. Somps tried to land a knock-out blow, but the Colonel either hugged the floor or clinched to save himself.

At the end of the second round Brady was still on his feet, demanding another round. As Somps had no objection the Colonel was given a "bracer" and time was again called. Somps landed a hard right on the jaw, which sent Brady to the floor in a dazed condition. He recovered before the ten seconds were up and started in to do his opponent A hot mix-up followed, in which the Colonel was again bent to the floor. After recovering from the effects of the blow, Brady complained that one of his gloves had been damaged in the fracas. He walked over to Somps and placing the glove under his nose asked Somps to examine it. Somps promptly dropped his arms. intending to look at the glove, when the foxy Colonel landed his right flush on the big fellow's solar plexus, and he fell as though he had been struck by a club in the hands of a south-of-Market-Street policeman.

For a time, it was thought he was fatally injured. He recovered, however. In a short time, much to the relief of Brady, who was momentarily expecting to be arrested for murder. The Colonel was awarded the fight and stakes, against the protest of Somps and his seconds. Brady's friends on account of the great victory are seriously thinking of matching him with the Sausalito Toothpick for a side bet of $1,000.

FELL FROM A CAR.
P. G. Somps Received Serious Injuries on Howard Street.

P. G. Somps, the well-known proprietor of steam soda works in this city, met with an accident Thursday afternoon that came near resulting in his death.

Shortly after 1 o'clock Mr. Somps, who is near 60 years of age, boarded a Howard-Street Car at Fourth and rode down to Third, where he intended to transfer to Montgomery.

There was me misunderstanding regarding the transfer and Mr. Somps argued with the conductor until the car had crossed Third Street. Unable to do business with the conductor Mr. Somps jumped from the car, which wan in motion. In doing so the old gentleman fell backward on the cobbles, landing on the back of his head. The fall tendered him unconscious, but the car sped away without stopping to investigate.

The injured man was picked up by a gentleman who saw the accident, and carried Mr. Somps into the drugstore on the corner. A doctor was sent for, and it took 20 minutes to restore Mr.

Somps to consciousness. He was then taken to bis home, at Twenty-Second and Mission Streets, where Dr. Bazet has seen in constant attendance ever since. The old gentleman is badly hurt in the rear of the head and back and suffers much pain. He is seriously injured, but it is thought he will recover.

August 20. 1902 San Francisco Call

GRACE BROS. BREWERIES, HISTORY & MEMORABILIA
SANTA ROSA - LOS ANGELES – SACRAMENTO - FRESNO

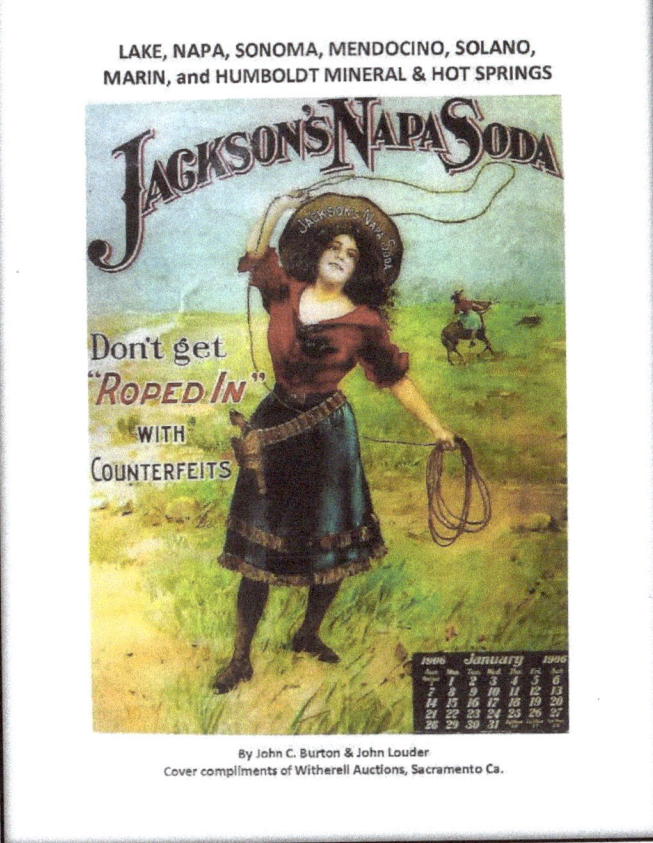

By John C. Burton

With Major Contributions by
Rawley Douglas
John Cartwright
James Arietta
Bob Welch
Cathy Grace-Hayes

LAKE, NAPA, SONOMA, MENDOCINO, SOLANO, MARIN, and HUMBOLDT MINERAL & HOT SPRINGS

By John C. Burton & John Louder
Cover compliments of Witherell Auctions, Sacramento Ca.

SAN RAFAEL - SAUSALITO – SAN ANSELMO
SODA, SELTZER, BEER, AND SPIRITS BOTTLES

A GUIDE AND REFERENCE TO BOTTLERS OF BEER, SODA, SELTZER,
AND SPIRITS OF MARIN COUNTY INCLUDING A LISTING OF ANTIQUE BOTTLES

By John C. Burton & John Louder

BOTTLES, TOKENS & HISTORY
OF
SONOMA COUNTY
May 2017

SODA, BEER, AND WHISKEY BOTTLES
FEATURING SALOON TOKENS

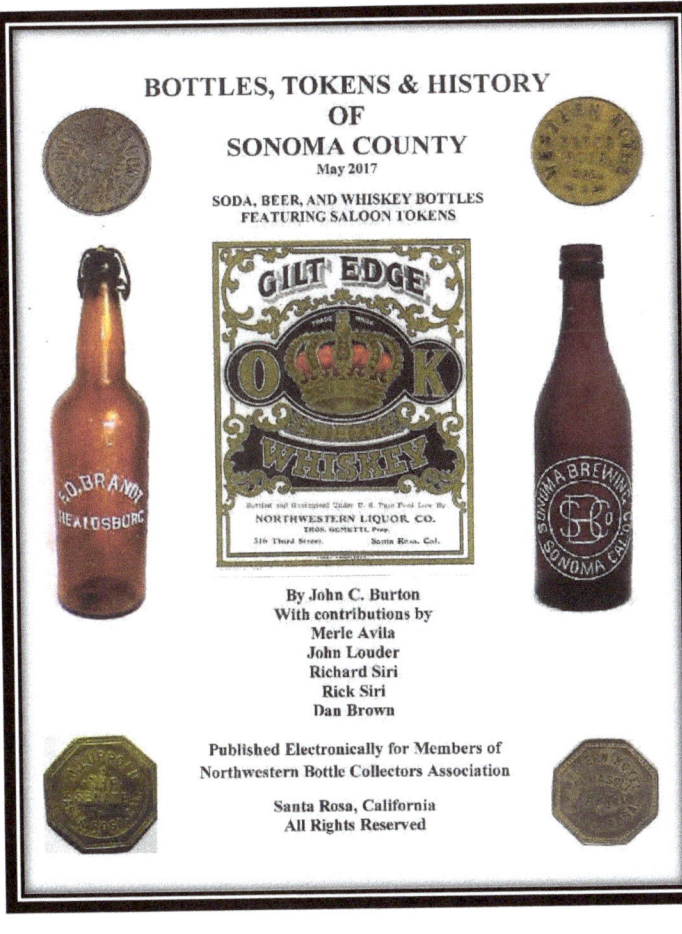

By John C. Burton
With contributions by
Merle Avila
John Louder
Richard Siri
Rick Siri
Dan Brown

Published Electronically for Members of
Northwestern Bottle Collectors Association

Santa Rosa, California
All Rights Reserved

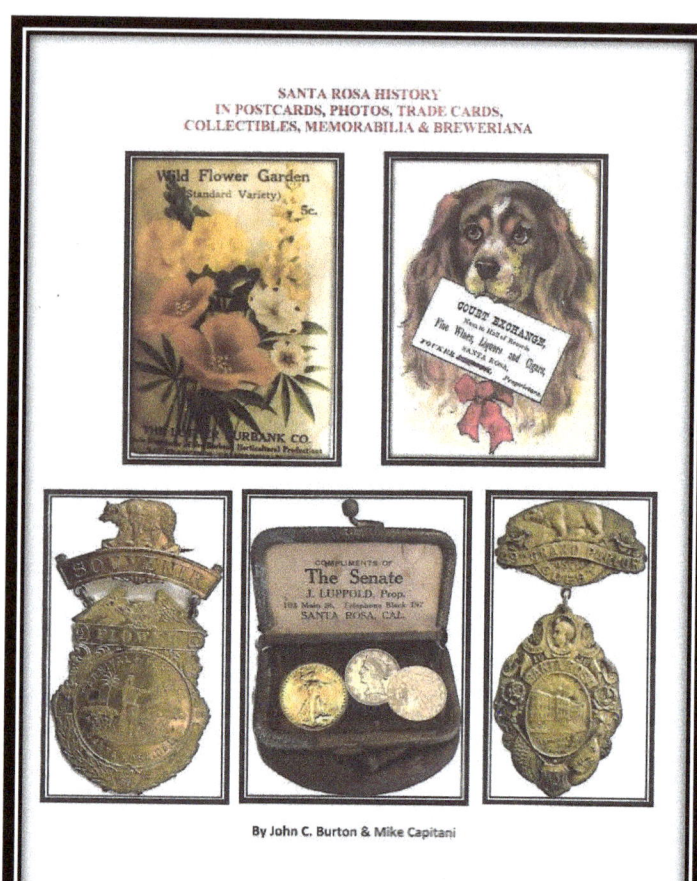

SANTA ROSA HISTORY
IN POSTCARDS, PHOTOS, TRADE CARDS,
COLLECTIBLES, MEMORABILIA & BREWERIANA

By John C. Burton & Mike Capitani

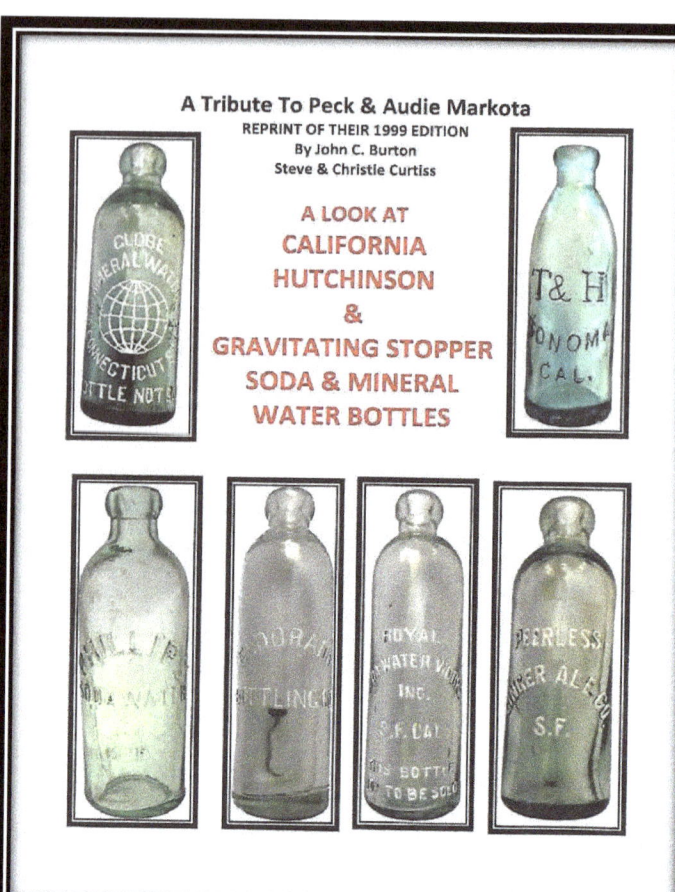

A Tribute To Peck & Audie Markota
REPRINT OF THEIR 1999 EDITION
By John C. Burton
Steve & Christie Curtiss

A LOOK AT
CALIFORNIA
HUTCHINSON
&
GRAVITATING STOPPER
SODA & MINERAL
WATER BOTTLES

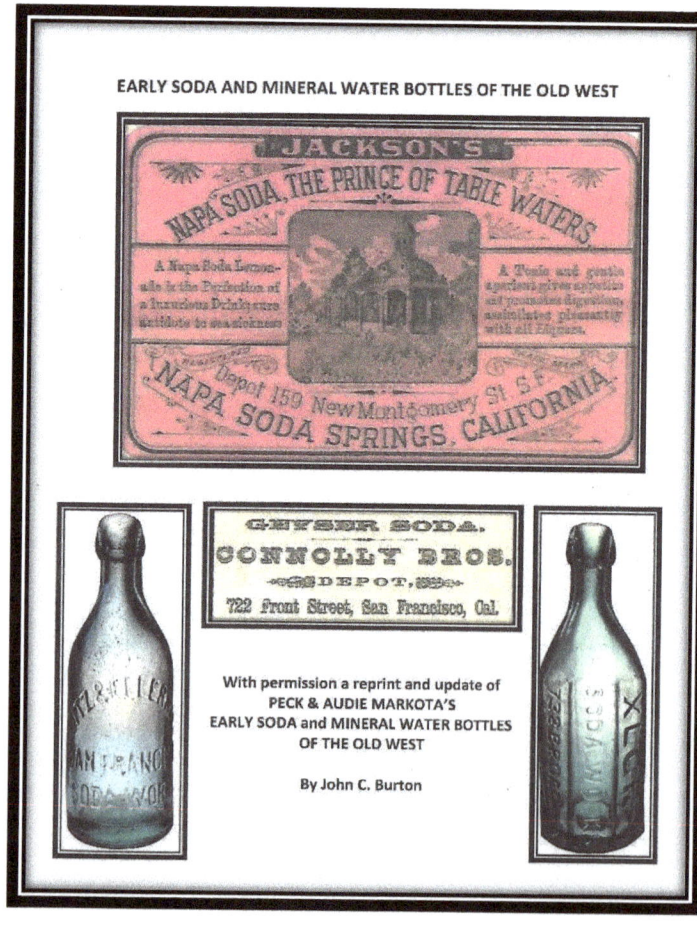

EARLY SODA AND MINERAL WATER BOTTLES OF THE OLD WEST

With permission a reprint and update of
PECK & AUDIE MARKOTA'S
EARLY SODA and MINERAL WATER BOTTLES
OF THE OLD WEST

By John C. Burton

WESTERN BEERS
BOTTLES, ADVERTISEMENT, LABELS,
PORCELAIN BOTTLE STOPPERS,
& HISTORY

Compiled By John C. Burton

SONOMA COUNTY DRUGGISTS

Featuring Advertising, Bottles, Medicine Glasses, Photographs and Local History

Maynard's Drug Store, Petaluma, circa 1900

Frank A. Sternad and John C. Burton

EARLY MEDICINE BOTTLES
OF THE
WESTERN FRONTIER

A Guide and Reference of Western Medicine Bottles

Republished by John C. Burton

SONOMA COUNTY BOTTLES, LABELS & BOTTLERS

By John C. Burton

SPLITS & THAT'S IT

A GUIDE AND REFERENCE TO PRE-PROHIBITION
CALIFORNIA HALF PINT BEER BOTTLES
BLOB TOPS, BALTIMORE LOOP & CROWN TOP BOTTLES
By Michael Burgess
Edited by John C. Burton

FINAL COCKTAIL BOOK
By John C. Burton

COCKTAIL BITTERS

APERITIFS – COCKTAILS – PUNCHES – HI-BALLS
TRADITIONAL RECIPES

Bartending BASICS

Everything You Need to Know to be a Working Bartender

JOHN C. BURTON

La Edición Revisada en Español

AMIGO DEL CANTINERO
Una Guia y Referencia para el Barman
Aprobado y Recomenandado Por
United States Bartender's Guild, California Chapter

John C. Burton   Salvador Sahagún

BOB WELCH COLLECTION OF CALIFORNIA
PRE-PROHIBITION, PROHIBITION AND CALIFORNIA PERMIT & IRTP PAPER BEER BOTTLES AND LABELS

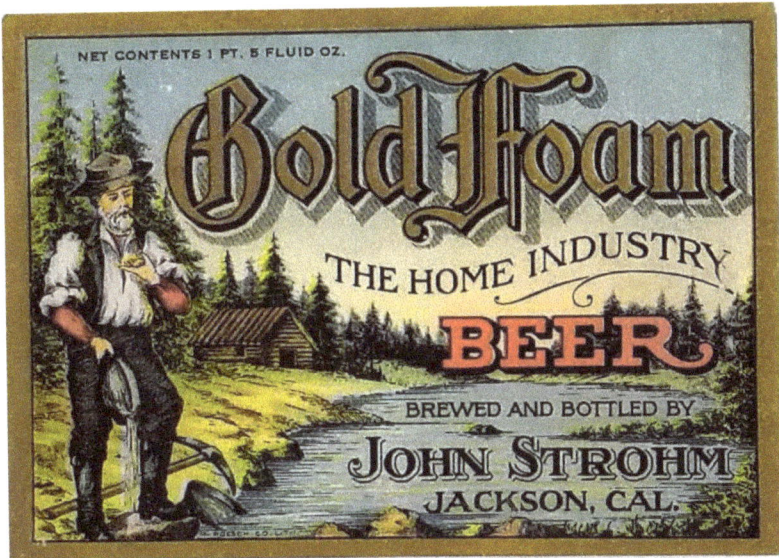

NET CONTENTS 1 PT. 5 FLUID OZ.

Gold Foam
THE HOME INDUSTRY
BEER
BREWED AND BOTTLED BY
JOHN STROHM
JACKSON, CAL.

NET CONTENTS 11 OZ. OR OVER.

EXCELSIOR
BEER
BREWED AND BOTTLED BY SANTA CRUZ BREWING CO.
SANTA CRUZ, CAL.

Compiled by John C. Burton
Bob Welch Collection